The MACADAMIA BRAIN

The 10 Principles To Build A Resilient And Tough Brain

SK LIOW

ISBN
Paperback 979-8-89673-440-6
Hardcase 979-8-89906-550-7

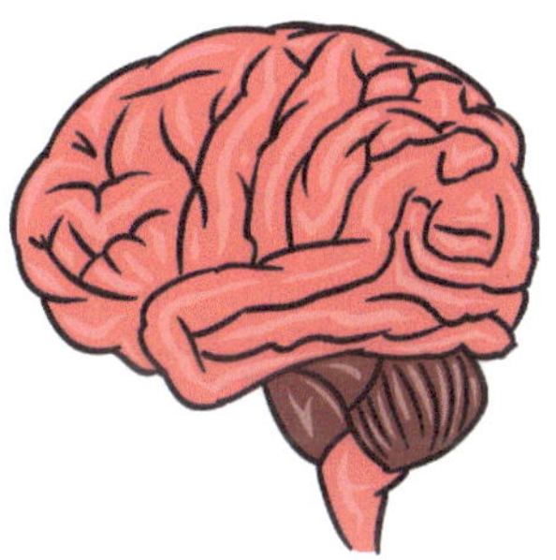

The Macadamia Brain:

How to toughen your mental resilience in the post-pandemic era of social media onslaught, megatrends of Generative AI, quantum computing, and blockchain revolution.

Positive psychology fortified by Physics, infused with stoicism and spiced up by ancient Asian philosophy - The *10 steps to Mental Fitness*, to thrive in the post-COVID-19 pandemic, and beyond…

By SK Liow (aka the Seize-the-Day guy)

To my parents,

for your immense love and sacrifice.

To my wife and daughter,

for the sheer joy and adventure,

In this amazing journey called LIFE.

Three Cheers to *Wabi-sabi*!

CONTENTS

INTRODUCTION

What has macadamia got to do with the brain? Well, there are 4 nutty reasons why I named the title of this eBook with the catchy phrase like *Macadamia Brain*. Firstly, the toughest nut to crack in the world is the macadamia nut. It takes a 300 pounds per square inch force to crack this amazing nut. No kidding! Secondly, macadamia nuts improve and protect our brain health[1] (think monounsaturated fats). The fat content is about 76%, which is the highest among nuts. Compared to almonds, it has a better omega-fat ratio. It has copper, magnesium, and manganese that help in the maintenance of healthy neurotransmitters in our brains. Thirdly, it is the most expensive nut in the world. And finally, it is my all-time favourite nut for a snack[2].

Now that we've got the mystery of the catchy title out of the way, let's dive into the contents. This book contains proven strategies and time-tested wisdom that aim to *toughen* up your brain and mindset, to cope with the post-COVID-19 era, and to thrive in spite of the challenges brought about by the new world order, including the AI revolution, blockchain, quantum computing, and other megatrends. And like the macadamia nut, the brain will be *tough to crack* once it embraces the fortifying techniques and protective systems that this book is going to talk about.

---

[1] I hear you, Walnut. But give some love for macadamia, too, chill?
[2] …and guess which is my favourite *Haagen-Dazs* pick? *Haagen-Dazs* Macadamia Nut!

Truth be told, *Life* can be one big mystery. Be it the wonders of the cosmos, our origins, the clashes of religious doctrines, the profound and inevitable impact of death, or whether Generative AI will overtake human intelligence, it is overwhelming at times. Indeed, over the centuries, we humans have started to evaluate these confounding questions and look for answers and clues.

Many schools of thought have emerged, ranging from supernatural, mystic, spiritual, and stoicism to humanistic and scientific discoveries. The advancements in psychological, sociological, and anthropological studies have also contributed immensely to the understanding of *homo sapiens* as a species.

The COVID-19 pandemic is *the* unprecedented game-changer and disrupter of this century. Without doubt, its pervasive and pernicious impact on mankind, from rich nations to poor nations, from huge corporations to the man on the street, has humbled us and made us all rethink and reflect on many of the traditional lifestyles and socio-economic models that have been developed over the years. Whilst Capitalism managed to recover from the *cardiac arrest* of the COVID-19 pandemic, our hectic rat-race life has also hit the pause button in so many ways, giving us time to contemplate and reflect on our journey in this life during the pandemic lockdown. Phrases like work-from-home and Zoom meetings are buzzwords used every other day. Also not spared is our mental health, given the social isolation and economic havoc directly caused by the mutating virus. Now, with the normalisation of international travel and cross-border relaxation, the *Why* question of the COVID-19 pandemic and its after-effects still lingers for many of us.

This book attempts to distil 10 powerful and proven techniques or systems that can help us to live our lives *optimally* in this challenging time, inoculate our brains against negativity, and even thrive in the post-pandemic era. It does not promise to answer all the philosophical questions staring at mankind. However, as they say, success leaves clues. Indeed, many self-help books have been written to share strategies and timeless wisdom. Some are of universal value, and some are localised to the cultural settings. Whichever it is, there are consistent themes and overlapping reaffirmations among them.

The 10 strategies or systems, once properly understood and effectively applied (read internalised) in our daily lives, will have a wonderful and meaningful impact on our lives. They are *interrelated* and mutually reinforcing, based on good science, and have been reaffirmed by eminent scholars and experts in various fields of endeavours. They work in my life, and I sincerely hope that you will benefit from them, too. I also had the privilege of sharing the 10 principles with young people via the Mental Fitness workshop (virtual and physical), which had just completed its 7th season since 2020. The numerous feedbacks from these young people have reaffirmed the amazing attributes and immense impact of these principles on making our mind-set more resilient.

According to 2021 scientific data[3], the COVID-19 pandemic will eventually become endemic, meaning we human beings will learn to live with it, using our immune system and antibodies as our shield and defence, so that we all can get on with our daily lives without the chronic fear of infection. The same is true for our lives' problems and challenges. What daily problems and challenges will be "endemic" in our lives so that we can use a resilient brain to tackle and rise above these issues?

Truth be told, the only categories of people who truly do not have any problems or challenges are those found 6 feet below the ground or those ashes found in the cremation vase/urn. Whilst all of us are alive, we *will* have problems and challenges, big or small. So, perspective-wise, be thankful that we have problems or challenges because it means *we are alive*! And I'll bet that many of those people 6 feet under the ground and those with ashes in the cremation vase/urn would be more than happy to trade places with us with all the problems just to be ALIVE! So, given that problems and challenges are part and parcel of living, it would be wonderful to be able to *vaccinate* our brains, to be tough like the macadamia nut, and to be able to tackle and overcome daily problems and challenges. This is where the 10 fortifying concepts in this book will be your mental *booster shots* to toughen up your brain to handle many of life's problems and challenges.

I have endeavoured to use a straightforward style of writing to convey the 10 amazing strategies to strengthen our minds and to inoculate our lives

---

3 World Economic Forum's article, dated 21 September 2021, written by Lara Herrero & Eugene Madzokere of Griffith University, Australia.

against the challenges and uncertainties caused by the COVID-19 pandemic and thereafter. Religiosity and political thoughts are kept at bay, being the 2 most divisive subjects, and at times beyond the norm of logic and reason. However, timeless wisdom and profound philosophy that has workable principles from Chinese culture, Japanese culture, and ancient Greek Stoicism will be peppered appropriately in the various topics in this book. That said, for the strategies to work, you need to understand it, *internalise* it and then *apply* it. It is like you have a rusty or worn-out saw and you are tired, and someone offered you a powerful brand-new turbo-charged electric saw. You can choose not to use it (because the old ways have *always* worked) or worse, you use it wrongly—by treating it as an axe or worse, a manual saw (imagine that). However, should you open your mind, embrace change, and learn how to *switch on the electric saw* (so to speak), the optimal life awaits you.

"The essence of knowledge is, having it, to apply it."
– Confucius.

Disclaimer: This eBook is intended to be an informational sharing and encouragement platform and is not intended to be a substitute for medical treatment where required. Should you have any mental stress and/or issues that require prompt medical attention, please seek appropriate medical help.

CHAPTER 1

MINDSET IS EVERYTHING

"A man is but the product of his thoughts. What he thinks, he becomes."
– Gandhi

The concept of mindset is so powerful that many of us have no idea how it can control and even direct our lives. The scientific community is only beginning to study and calibrate the *direct* correlation between the dynamics of mindset and the manifested improved quality of life in the last few decades.

It was Dr. Carol Dweck[4] who actually conducted a systematic study on this phenomenal area and shared the profound impact it had on early childhood and even working adults. Previously, there was an open debate as to whether we were just engaging in *wishful thinking* or dismissing any such concept as hocus-pocus, intangible, and pure conjecture. In fact, Dr. Dweck discovered that we all have different beliefs about the underlying nature of ability. The good news is that consistent study and independent peer review among the scientific community have proven the measurable and significant impact mindset will have on how we think, behave, solve problems, and live our daily lives. Indeed, it has a confounding influence on whether we are happy, sad, challenged, defeated, or victorious in our outlook on life.

There are a lot of applications in the field of mindset. The growth mindset versus stagnated mindset, the curious mind versus the know-it-all mind, the

---

4 *Mindset: The New Psychology of Success* (2007) by Dr. Carol Dweck, Professor of Psychology at Stanford University.

contrasting effect of the scarcity mindset versus the abundance mindset, and the difference between finite and infinite mindset are some of the popular ones. Understanding these contrasting mindsets will help us to see whether we have limiting mindsets or empowering mindsets, and the desire and conscious effort to change our mindsets will propel us into a whole new living dimension. Dr. Dweck propounded that children (and adults, too) with a *growth* mindset believe that intelligence and abilities can be developed through effort, persistence, grit, and learning from mistakes along the way.

Speaking of a limiting mindset, some of us may have heard of Roger Bannister. He was the Cambridge University medical student who smashed the 4-minute barrier in the good old one-mile race. You see, in 1954, the Imperial measurement system (inch, feet, yard, mile, etc.) was the prevailing system (and not the Metric system), and they had this one-mile race (about 1.6 km) as one of the seminal track and field events. The *established* scientific fact from the *experts* then (up to 1954) was that it was humanly *impossible* to run the one-mile race below 4 minutes. No way. The human body was not designed to run below the 4-minute time. The lungs' capacity, the way our physiology was built, and our legs, etc, all demonstrated that we were not able to break the 4-minute barrier. And sure enough, nobody could—thereby confirming the *established* scientific *fact* then. So, a limiting mindset leads to a limiting outcome. *But* Roger Bannister refused to believe that. He believed that it *could* be broken.

Well, Roger Bannister trained hard for it, and on that historic day of May 6th, 1954, he ran the mile in 3 minutes and 59.4 seconds. What a shocker! He became the first man to break the *impossible* 4 minutes, and the world woke up to this seminal breakthrough in the track and field arena. Nice, Roger became a legend and was knighted as Sir Roger Gilbert Bannister CH CBE FRCP. But that's not the best part. That record of 3 minutes and 59.4 seconds was broken in just 46 days by John Landy in Australia (3 minutes and 58 seconds). Then, about 12 months later, the 4-minute was broken by another 3 runners, all in a *single race*. Today, thousands of runners have convincingly smashed the 4-minute barrier. So much for *established* physiological facts then. Why? Because the *impossible* has been rephrased to *I'm possible*.

For contextual mindset illustration, imagine a 5-year-old boy or girl from England telling his or her mum that he or she wants to be the fastest sprinter in the world right after the sensational victory by Roger Bannister. His or her parents would certainly take him or her seriously. That same boy or girl, if he or she was born in Jamaica in 1954, would probably have made his or her parents tickled pink, and that's about it. But move the timeline to 2009, when the legendary Usain Bolt set the world record for the 100-metre race in Berlin at 9.58 seconds. Now, those same parents would start making calls for a coach!

When I was a young student, I did well in my primary 1, and my primary school then decided to group all the top 10 students in every primary class to be in the *express* class and crammed primary 2 and 3 years into a one-year study. It was a complete disaster for me, academically speaking. Presumably because I was a *slow learner* then. It was a perfect recipe for regression—put a slow learner in an express class! I ended up almost at the bottom of the express class, and my personal confidence took a beating for years. Getting my dad to sign my annual school report was a challenge with all the low marks in my subjects. In secondary school, I then gradually improved my grades when I picked up reading as a hobby, and I also secured a 2nd-rank class, missing the 1st-rank class by a small margin. This makes me the one-eye-jack in the land of the blind, so to speak, in the 2nd-rank class. Hell, I was the top student in the 2nd-rank class. This gave me gradual confidence and nurtured my mindset to embrace learning heartily. The next thing I knew, I became the top debater (in public debate) in my school, and later went on to do a double degree in Psychology and Law at one of the top universities in Australia[5].

It was also during this turnaround period of academic progress that I remembered reading a remarkable paperback book with an eye-catching title called *You Can If You Think You Can* by Norman Vincent Peale (1974). I bought the book from a humble bookshop (Union Bookshop, if I recall the name) in my quaint hometown called Alor Star[6]. It blew my mind. I recall it as one of my first self-help or self-improvement books that made me fall in love with all the subsequent self-improvements that I read over the years, even until now. The title was catchy and captivated me (especially given my many disempowering beliefs then). Reading that book opened the can-do mindset in me and allowed me to venture into many learning areas and wonderful explorations in my life. Over the years, I have read many other profound and life-changing books (by famous authors such as Dr. Stephen Covey, Anthony

---

[5] Australian National University, Canberra (BA [Psychology] 1984; LLB 1986)

[6] Capital of Kedah, up north of Peninsular Malaysia.

Robbins, Robin Sharma, and many others) that challenged and transformed my limiting mindset.

Another explosive mindset breakthrough in learning, understanding, and memory retention is in the area of *how* we learn. Most traditional teaching and writing styles were very much linear until the *mind-map* proponent Tony Buzan[7] came along. He had great difficulty in learning when he was a young student in the UK. Then, he discovered the creative way of learning through mind-mapping interconnection with multiple colours, associations, and visual/graphic illustrations. It not only catapulted him into a brilliant student who was not just effective in learning, understanding, and retention but also revolutionised many of the learning institutional approaches in countries all over the world. Some years back, I had the privilege of meeting him when he was still alive and had come over to Kuala Lumpur for a mind-mapping talk. In fact, the concept of mind mapping (or its variant styles) was already being used or adopted by great thinkers such as Leonardo da Vinci and Albert Einstein in their various problem-solving endeavours.

The essential ingredients to the concept of mind mapping are key ideas, connected branches, distinctive colours, keywords, and vivid images. Granted, we all learn differently. However, there are common learning patterns. Take the letters e, l, e, p, h, a, n, and t. Once we learn how to arrange and spell elephant, we no longer think of the letters individually, but the concept and/or the mental/visual image of an elephant is already prefixed in our mind. But it is still rather linear. Mind Map takes it to a whole new level, using visuals, differing colours, associations, branches/sub-branches, and connections to deepen our 3D holistic understanding of concepts and problems. And because of its emphasis on visualisation, it helps our brain not just to grasp the big picture of many issues, but where planning is involved, it also aids us to see our goals and issues in more concrete terms. It is enormously useful for complex planning and brainstorming ideas, scenario-buildings, and even goal setting. I have enjoyed using it for problem-solving with clients and even for court trial preparations and strategies. So long as we are open to learning, ideas abound around us.

---

7 Anthony Peter "Tony" Buzan (1942-2019), a British author and educational consultant.

"The only true wisdom is in knowing you know nothing."
– Socrates

Speaking of learning, Matt Keller wrote a book with the rather audacious title *"The Key to Everything"*[8], with the catchy sub-line *"Unlocking the secret to why some people succeed, and others don't."* Guess what is *the* key? According to Keller, it is *teachability*, and his formula for your level of teachability is the desire to learn multiplied by the willingness to change, i.e., adaptability. Teachability is not something that some people are born with, and others aren't, but it is a characteristic that can be learned and grown. This amplifies the teachability mindset already articulated by the great Confucius[9] thousands of years ago when he expounded that by walking among 3 people, I *will* find my teacher among them. I choose that which is good in them and follow it, and that which is bad and change it. 子曰：[三人行，必有我師焉。擇其善者而從之，其不善者而改之.] This literally means that *anyone* can be my teacher and that I can learn from anyone. That is teachability at an expanding mindset level and humility in learning. A fantastic mindset to have!

The contrasting effect of the learning or growth mindset versus the know-it-all mindset has a profound effect on our *progress* or *regress* in learning, and how enriching or one-dimensional our lives would eventually become. The famous Chinese sayings like *"no limit to learning"* [学无止境] and *"live until old age, learn until old age"* [活到老，学到老] truly epitomise the imperative of continuous thirst for knowledge and learning. When was the last time you looked up the dictionary (physical or digital) for the definition of a new word or even relooked at the definition of any word taken for granted?

The good news is this: The Science of *Neuroplasticity* has debunked the old *established* biological view that our brain stops growing upon adolescence and that our brain will continue to grow and change all the way through adulthood. In fact, our brain will continue to learn and *adapt* according to life experiences! Conversely, if we don't use our brain, it will regress. *Neurogenesis* is the term used to describe the process by which new neurons are formed in our brain. Previously, it was thought that neurogenesis took place during embryonic development, and growth is observed until part of the early adolescent years. However, since the advancement of neuroscience in

---

8 Matthew William Keller, 2015, Published by Nelson Books.
9 Chinese Philosopher (551 BC - 479 BC)

the last few decades, it is now accepted that neurogenesis can even occur in the hippocampi of adult brains, and even in the amygdala[10]. Here's a fun and exciting tip: aerobic activities like walking, running, hiking, swimming, and cycling can effectively boost neurogenesis. Why? This is because when the heart is pumping continuously at the hyper-oxygenation level for more than 20 minutes, several growth hormones are then elevated in our brain[11].

Ancora Imparo (I am still learning)
Michelangelo Buonarroti
(Italian artist, 1475-1564)
(Wrote this at the age of 87)

So, exactly *how* do we learn? Aristotle's analysis of learning memory talks about the *4 laws of association*, viz., the law of contiguity, contrast, frequency, and similarity. And the approach is called Associationism. He was possibly the first recorded scholar to frame the learning memory in terms of laws of association. Two intriguing concepts are worth highlighting here. One is the law of Contiguity, which basically means that after events occur together (in spatio-temporal proximity), the reoccurrence of only one event can trigger the memory of the others. This law of contiguity is accepted as the fundamental premise of scientific theories of learning, memory, and knowledge. The other is the concept of association.

The law of contiguity is remarkable. The thing to note is this, the more intense or vivid the first event, the more the memory will retain (or rather *burnt* into your neurons). Ask yourself—where were you when the 9-11 tragedy hit the New York Twin Towers in 2001? Most of you would have no problem recalling it; in fact, you will recall it quite vividly. But ask yourself again, where were you on 9-12 or 9-13 of 2001? You get my point.

There are also related strategies we can learn in optimising our mental fitness by harnessing the law of contiguity and the law of association. In practical terms, if we create a *conducive* environment for studying, reading, or learning a manual skill, then if we can regularly sustain that ideal environment

---

[10] Discovery in 1992 by Professors Perry Bartlett and Linda Richards.
[11] See Chapter 4 on this exciting topic of body-brain interconnection.

for our intended task, our focus and productivity are much easier to achieve. This creates the optimal and inviting habitat for us to learn efficiently. So, things like pleasant background music, well-circulated air, decluttered space (i.e., minimal distractions), and empowering quotes on the surrounding wall are fantastic for a productive study environment.

And precisely because of the powerful influence of *association* with the way our brain works, the advertising world has brilliantly tapped into this connection to lure consumers to buy the advertised products. Millions of fees are paid to the gorgeous actress Nicole Kidman and the advertising company for her to just do a 2-minute short film that associates her with *Chanel No. 5*. How does it work? Simply because at the basal level, the association is how our brain works (or rather learns). So, subliminally, buying and using Chanel No. 5 is wonderful for me because if superstar Nicole Kidman endorses it or is using it (*and* she is a beautiful, glamorous, and successful actress), when I buy and use Chanel No. 5, I am also *associated* with Nicole Kidman subliminally, which would then *invoke* the aura of beauty, glamour, and success around me, somehow. The irrefutable magic of association is so powerful that Coco Chanel's company even got Brad Pitt to do the *Chanel No. 5* advertisement for the men's version. As the tagline goes, it is not just a scent but a timeless symbol of desire. Word on the street is that every 30 seconds, a *Chanel No. 5* is sold somewhere in the world. See the power of association on display here?

However, when the law of association is misapplied in our social-dynamic daily living, it can be comical and sometimes even create cultural taboos. In Chinese culture, it is the unspoken rule that if you attend a funeral, then you should not attend a wedding thereafter on the same day (or even within the next few days), and *vice versa*. Why? Because it is being *disrespectful* or that the visit to one event will bring *bad luck* to the other event or venue (aka taboo). Could it be that some of the tiny dust from the funeral would be picked up and brushed off at the wedding, thereby causing misfortune to the bride and groom? From an objective scientific perspective, you know the answer. But from the sociological or cultural context, it will create a *heated* debate. That, my friend, is the law of association at play. Our mind is indeed a marvellous thing—it can brilliantly land a man on the moon, but it can also *reason* that going to the wedding after a funeral is a no-no. In this sense, we need to remove our objective scientific glasses and put on our sociological lens with the aid of the understanding of the law of association; then the context makes more sense and the picture will be clearer and more tolerated. Mindset is rather multi-dimensional at times when cultural norms and taboos blur the rational mind or when superstition hijacks logic.

Now, imagine you are caught in a sudden chill in Melbourne, one of the most liveable cities in the world, which has the unique *4 seasons in a day* phenomenon. And you are not properly suited up with a warm jacket. I am offering you 2 identical warm jackets, one of which has been used by Adolf Hitler before and the other by Mother Teresa. Which one would you choose to wear? Instinctively, we would choose Mother Teresa's jacket. Why? Because the law of association is working here. Would wearing Hitler's jacket make you evil, or would wearing Mother Teresa's jacket make you more giving and gracious? The metaphysical dynamics here are as real as it gets. It is as though the aura of Hitler would somehow rub onto you or be assimilated into your mind or body, and influence you or the DNA of Mother Teresa would somehow be absorbed into your epidermis or your outer skin and seep into your consciousness or soul/being.

At the physical level, the 2 warm apparel would do none of that, the thick fabric or woollen materials on either apparel stay where they are, with absolutely no organic interaction with our epidermis or body, apart from retaining the body heat and shielding the external cold, which would then keep us warm. But the mind's perception of the association of the apparel—it is a whole different level. That is the mindset at play. Now, change the scenario. I teleport you to the South Pole with your thin Hawaiian shirt now. The temperature is sub-sub-zero at -50°C. Then, I offer you *only* Hitler's thick jacket as extra apparel to keep your body warm so that you would not freeze to death. The survival instinct kicks in; the mind says it is JUST a jacket—who cares if the previous owner had slaughtered millions of Jews during WW2?

Recent studies have also firmly confirmed the amazing power of mindset, even over the physiological changes to our body[12]. Dr. Alia Crum's exciting TED Talk (*Change your Mindset, Change your Game*, 2014) where she shared how we missed the elephant in the room, viz. the placebo. Dr. Alia Crum shared about the various placebo-effect experiments, and how with the empowering and encouraging mindset, the body *will* respond positively,

---

[12] See also the chapter on **Body-Mind Connection.**

and conversely; it would also create havoc with a disempowering mindset. Well, the jury is back, and good science has now confirmed the measurable psychosomatic connection between the brain and the physiological body and that *positive thinking*, which had been previously brushed off as wishful thinking, is indeed a powerful mental strategy and asset in living the optimal life.

The *placebo*[13] *effect* was studied in 1996 through a painkiller called Trivaricaine[14] to test the pain-easing properties on the participants' fingers, except that it was *not* a painkiller but a fake mixture with no pain-easing properties. Yet, the participants reported that the treated finger hurt significantly less than the untreated finger. Since the 18th century, placebo has been used on patients after the understanding that false drugs *can* improve patients' symptoms. It further became a useful tool in clinical trials to see if patients are truly exhibiting significant benefits from the clinical drug as compared to the placebo. To further minimise the confirmation bias, sometimes even the person who administers the drug was not told which drug was the placebo and which was the real McCoy; this is called the double-blind placebo. And many times, the results demonstrated the confounding effect of a placebo. The takeaway message is that the placebo effect is real, and this has to do with our mindset that our brain can *hack* our neurological and physiological responses to many external stimuli. OMG! This is more than brownie points for Positive Psychology.

The ever-energetic Mr. Why guy, Anthony Robbins (my hero), talks about how it is the *meaning* and *interpretation* we give to the events around our lives that decide our joy, stress, and other range of emotions, and eventually shape the destiny of our lives. Therefore, we need to carefully choose the appropriate meaning and response to all these events and circumstances. This is *why* having a positive, healthy, and growing mindset is a *compelling* reason to tackle the many ups and downs of life.

The English management strategist and modern thinker, Simon Sinek, has been developing and sharing the idea of the finite and infinite mindsets. Powerful mindset stuff. As we grow up, we learn to *compare* through

---

13 In Latin, it literally means "I shall please".
14 Mechanism of Placebo Pain Reduction: An Empirical Investigation (1996) by Guy Montgomery & Irving Kirsch

friendly competitions, sports events, and school rankings. In a sense, society needs to streamline skills and abilities for better *productivity* (read: for the eventual benefits of the corporate industrialists and national productivity). So, from a young age, we pick up this somewhat unhealthy habit of comparison. Now, comparison *per se* is not the enemy. It is the effect it has on our individuality, self-worth, and mindset that is harmful. Psychologists use the term *reference anxiety* to describe such a stress creator. The key problem with comparison is that if you compare with people who are better than you, you feel lousy, and conversely, if you compare with people who are worse than you, you feel better. So, *why* you compare and *how* you compare can be manipulated and will have a determining influence on your mood and self-worth.

Interestingly, it has been observed that invariably bronze medallists are happier and more satisfied than the silver medallists in any Olympics competition. Why? Psychologists call this a manifestation of *Counterfactual Thinking*. The bronze medallist says to himself or herself, "Phew! At least I managed to get a medal...," but the self-talk[15] of the silver medallist is: "If only I had got the Gold..." or "Aiyo[16]! How could I have missed the Gold!" And yet, ranking-wise, the silver medallist had measurably performed better than the bronze medallist. Indeed, the takeaway message is contextual framing or reframing of our mindset can directly affect our happiness and mental well-being.

"I never lose. I either win or learn."
– Nelson Mandela

As social animals, we consciously and unconsciously compare ourselves to others, visually, from height, weight, and beauty to financial matters like cars, houses, clothes, spouses, etc. Where it gets pernicious is the impact it has on our mindset and self-esteem. They say that there is no end to comparison, and depending on who you compare with, it can make you feel *superior* or *inferior*, which does not benefit your inner confidence and self-esteem in so many ways. I have given the following hypothetical scenarios to my workshop participants on mental fitness:

---

[15] See Chapter 5 on this powerful topic.
[16] Recognised by the Oxford English Dictionary since 2016, used to express distress, regret, or grief.

Scenario A: Imagine you and your 5 friends are employed by company A, and all your friends will be offered £1,600.00 per month, but only you will get £1,800.00 per month, and

Scenario B: Imagine you and your 5 friends are employed by company A, and all your friends will be offered £2,200.00 per month, but only you will get £2,000.00 per month.

Most participants will go for Scenario A, even though Scenario B offers a *higher* quantum every month. This is because, intrinsically and sociologically, we don't feel good in Scenario B. We can reason that we choose Scenario A because we are more capable, but the converse thinking would be that we then would feel inferior or not so capable in Scenario B. We will even defend our decision by arguing that salary is a function of our capability and experiences, etc. However, if you are able to remove yourself from any sense of comparison, then clarity dictates that Scenario B would financially benefit you better. *Social comparison can be as real as it gets*. And as social beings, it is difficult to have zero comparisons. In some ways, it is useful to find out where we are in our *station in life* and to see how we are progressing as compared to the rest of the cluster, community, or society. The stress comes in when we programme or give feedback to our mind that we are *not that good* when we are ranked lower than the rest of the group or more *superior* when we are at the top of the food chain, so to speak.

Let's go back to your 5 friends again. The trend is to wear certain premium brand clothing or an expensive watch or to own a certain premium smartphone. The peer pressure is real. You have a choice to join in, but your budget is an issue. You can either squeeze your budget and be in the trend, or buy less expensive clothing, a watch, or a smartphone, and allocate the balance to a long-term investment or help a worthy cause. Again, in this scenario, without social comparison and the toxic peer pressure, clarity and the value system in your life get a boost.

In some schooling systems, there is no ranking in class for the first few years, and everyone just enjoys learning *at their own pace*.[17] This

---

[17] Check out the Kumon system, as mentioned on page xx of the Kaizen concept.

minimises the stigmatisation and prejudicial treatment against weak/slow students and the over-glorification of brilliant students. If the mindset of the teacher is that there is a genius in *every* child to be tapped and discovered, then the teaching approach is that of optimising the unique human potential, rather than just unloading passive information to the class based on the bell-curve approach, viz. the one-size-fits-all for the average student. Sir Ken Robertson[18] from the UK is trying to revolutionise the way we have been approaching the fundamentals of education, and he draws emphasis on the uniqueness of every student to be tapped, and that IQ has been overrated. His TED Talk since 2007 has drawn millions of views, and people are seriously rethinking the conventional ways we have been approaching the education methodology.

Back to the finite and infinite mindset, if you take the popular sports of badminton or tennis, you have 2 competing players (or 4 players if you are playing doubles), you will have a scoring system, and you will eventually have a winner and a loser. It is finite, and there is a beginning and an end. All in good fun, unless you have become aggressively competitive. Then you will *only* accept winning, and allow losing to give you negative feedback, which then becomes harmful. In your daily life, what if you just *compete* with yourself, in the sense of aiming to improve your skills, knowledge or productivity outputs on a daily basis without habitual reference to others? There is no scoring board, and there is no endpoint. The correct mindset here would be that we are truly a work in progress. There is no need to compare; while peace and tranquillity permeate our minds, progress becomes more natural and organic. This is where the daily nurturing of **Kaizen** comes in…

---

[18] Do Schools Kill Creativity - 7th Jan 2007 By Sir Ken Robinson.

CHAPTER 2

KEEP CALM AND KAIZEN ON…

Life can be overwhelming. Problems seem insurmountable at times. Whatever mindset we have, sometimes we still don't seem to overcome the issues. There is, however, a wonderful *brain-hack* technique that we can use to counter such *overwhelming* obstacles. It is called *Kaizen*.

It is a Japanese word that literally means gracious change for the better (in Chinese, the translation of the 2 characters literally means gracious change [改善]). Conceptually, it entails the idea of *incremental* and *continuous* improvement.

As a matter of fact, this book is made possible because of the concept of Kaizen[19]. One sentence at a time, one paragraph at a time, one chapter at a time, and *voilà*, it gets completed eventually. They say that the way to eat an elephant is *one bite at a time*. Figure of expression. In case there are vegans out there, the way to eat a pumpkin is also one bite at a time.

One of the marvellous benefits of Kaizen is its ability to *counter* inertia and lethargy. You see, our mind will instinctively feel overwhelmed when the task at hand is *too difficult* or *onerous*, and the sense of being overwhelmed paralyses us into inaction and excuse-seeking mode. However, when we intentionally and mindfully break the project or mission into mini-tasks and micro-steps, the brain then gets the message that it is so doable, that it is almost effortless, and hence the action to execute the mini-task is set in motion without further ado. Kaizen! Baby steps, and eventually, the *momentum* is built up, and the next thing we know, we have completed the marathon, scaled the peak of a

---

[19] The other reason is **Wabi-sabi**. Check it out in Chapter 10.

mountain, or completed a herculean assignment. In fact, in my younger days, I used to hike mountains, and I remember that it was just *one step at a time in the direction of the peak*. I told myself that the trick was to enjoy the process, and of course, reaching the peak was exhilarating (and exhausting!). Indeed, it is the journey that counts.

Interestingly, I have conducted numerous mental fitness workshops on these 10 concepts over the years for young people. When it comes to the Kaizen topic, I would delightfully ask for a volunteer to stand up, walk and touch the wall a few metres up the hall or lecture theatre and come back to the seat. He or she would happily and willingly perform it without asking the *why* and perhaps wondering what I was up to. Then I (with a straight face) would ask him or her to now proceed with the 42 km [20] run, and the group would all wait for him or her. Without fail, he or she would give me the *"wait-a-minute, are-you-kidding-me"* look. This has been the case *every* time I did the impromptu and unrehearsed experiment. You see, when the task is broken into a mini doable step, even the *why* question can be handled later. This does not stress the brain. But when the 42 km marathon task is entrusted upon them on the spot, the brain feels overwhelmed and immediately goes into a freeze mode. The illustration is extreme, but it showcases how our brain processes doable and overwhelming tasks.

In fact, that is exactly how one trains for any long-distance event—start small, build endurance, and gradually improve the metres to km, and the next thing you know, the finish line is just in front. I have personally trained and scaled the tallest peak in West Malaysia[21], and the tallest peak[22] in East Malaysia, and my mantra has always been *one step at a time, in the direction of the peak*. In the end, Kaizen is more concerned with the incremental process rather than being *obsessed* with the finish line. Indeed, the Kaizen mindset is not a finite mindset but an infinite mindset—meaning continuous incremental improvement. The mantra here is *work-in-progress*. That was how Toyota gradually overtook GM in the global auto landscape.

This brings to mind the 3Ms[23] that I advocate in my mental fitness workshops, viz. Motivation-Movement-Momentum. You ask, which one comes

---

[20] The approximate distance for a marathon.
[21] Gunung Tahan, Pahang - 2,187 metres/7,175 feet.
[22] Mount Kinabalu, Sabah – 4,095metres/13,435 feet.
[23] The resemblance with the *Minnesota Mineral & Mining* is coincidental.

first? Traditionally, it has been said that until and unless we are motivated, nothing moves. And if nothing moves, forget about momentum. And no momentum, no motivation. One vicious cycle. Inertia locks in. In fact, a lot of wannabe writers are still *waiting* for the *right* motivation or inspiration to come along before they embark on writing. However, if we change our *mindset* to allocate *equal* importance to movement, that movement can fuel or energise motivation, which then refuels movement, thereby generating momentum. (And momentum can also sustain motivation as well as movement.) To use the analogy of *fake it till you make it*, you are moving (activities) as if you are motivated, and the movement encourages your mind to crystallise and *sustain* the motivation. Anthony Robbins' message of *physiology* impacting our psychology fits in our discussion here—that physiological movement (good posture and intentional body movement) can alter psychological state.

The graphic illustration below helps to reframe our mindset about motivation and movement. Instead of the linear sequencing of motivation being the default precursor of movement and momentum, *any* one of the 3 components *can* be the initiator. With this circular mindset, we optimise the intention of *continuous* progress, given that it is sustained more effectively in a mutually reinforcing spiralling growth. For those martial artist students who are familiar with the beautiful *Aikido* [24] philosophy, the fluid, circular movement is the most elegant and graceful movement in the practice of this beautiful Japanese martial art. The same principle applies here. And applying the principle of Kaizen, the doable small movements, will help to create momentum and fuel motivation.

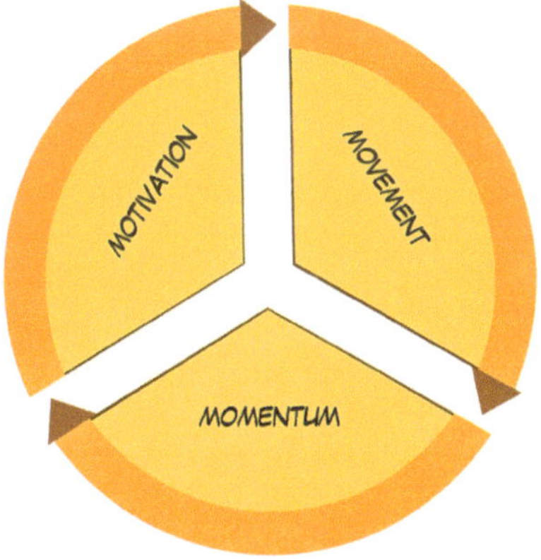

---

[24] Literally means the harmony of chi.

One of the often-quoted wisdom is *1% inspiration and 99% perspiration* by Thomas Alva Edison. He is the world-famous inventor who invented the lightbulb and phonograph, among many other inventions and patents. The takeaway message is that you have to work hard and 'not wait for inspiration to get you there. It's good wisdom. There is no substitute for deep work and diligence. Edison was a smart guy, extremely curious, and unbelievably tenacious in his many experiments. Also, that quote was said during the formative period of the so-called Industrial Revolution, where hard work, industrial long hours, and manual productivity were worshipped. In fact, Edison is credited today for helping to build America's economy during the Industrial Revolution. Nevertheless, as our society evolved, and modernisation transformed our standard of living, technological tools provided more leverage and efficiency, and *working smart* became the preferred buzzword to merely working hard. And in this aspect, Kaizen is the *leverage* in the mental tools of efficiency.

"Opportunity is missed by most people because it is dressed in overalls and it looks like work."
– Thomas Edison

In a sense, Thomas' mantra of "1% inspiration, 99% perspiration"[25] demotes motivation and glorifies hard and persistent work/labour. In this regard, many people often get discouraged or daunted by the seemingly insurmountable task at hand or are unable to get the momentum without inspiration or motivation. This is where Kaizen can be the *WD-40*[26], the wonder lubrication/degreaser/corrosion inhibitor to propel and sustain the spiral of the 3M! In a brain-hack context, once the brain sees the mini-tasks as doable and achievable, the sense of being overwhelmed is diminished, and the excitement kicks in, which fuels the movement, which in turn creates momentum. Try it in your daily tasks, from household chores to huge office projects, and see the astounding effect of Kaizen.

Take the case of your home. The urge to declutter your house or apartment may be inspired or motivated by some recent YouTube videos advocating the minimalist lifestyle, or you may be excited by *Marie Kondo's* joy threshold

---

[25] Actual Quote is "Genius is one percent inspiration and ninety-nine percent perspiration".
[26] Multi-purpose lubricant spray, degreaser and rust remover – produced by Rocket Chemical Company from USA.

to overhaul your wardrobe. But the sheer clutter in the garage, or the visual clutter of things and stuff surrounding you, would invariably paralyse you into inaction or procrastination. With inspiration diminished, there is no movement and no momentum. Well, Kaizen says to start with *one item* in your nearest accessible drawer. That's it. Get one item of clutter out and discard it. Mini victory. Celebrate. And watch your brain warm up to the momentum. I have personally experienced it in decluttering my house, and Kaizen was the prime reason why my wife and I are enjoying more space and visual calmness in our home now.

There is another motivational hack that propounds that the first thing we should do in the morning is to fold our blanket once we wake up. Very popular in military training. I used to not fold my blanket when I woke up, thinking to myself, "What's the point, as I will be using it again tonight." However, that simple act of mindfully folding the blanket will propel your brain to subconsciously build momentum for the rest of the day—one down, next to go, and you will be pleased that your bed looks neat and tidy, which improves your self-esteem. Celebrate the mini-wins and Kaizen in action.

Interestingly, James Clear, in his bestselling book *Atomic Habits,* talks about the 1% continuous improvement, which he called *The Power of Tiny Gains*[27]. In the Kaizen mindset, we are training our minds to continuously think of small *achievable* improvements, hence the term *continuous incremental improvement.* The resistance to this approach is the conventional wisdom or subliminal messages of *Think Big, Quantum Leap,* or *Make a Big Impact* mantras, which are more thrilling and make the 1% improvement relatively unglamorous and somewhat insignificant. The other compounding problem is the media's sensationalising of any individual or organisational achievement as an *overnight success*, which many of us know to be untrue as it takes relentless practice, perseverance, and grit to achieve long-lasting success. So, because of the subliminal message of *overnight success* or that so-and-so became an overnight sensation or hit the jackpot, we get turned off by the unglamorous mantra of *slow and steady*, we become impatient, and often attempt *shortcuts* to then achieve the illusive *overnight success*. So, the adage *Rome was not built in a day* is a wonderful reminder here.

The good news is that documented behavioural studies and psychological analysis have proven that the 1% improvement is more effective in terms

---

27 *Atomic Habits*, By James Clear (2018)

of *long-term sustained* success or a worthy endeavour. The trite old saying "*slow and steady wins the race*" is the effective mantra, after all! Even for top sprinters in the 100-metre events, if you observe carefully, the first stretch from the starting block is usually an explosive burst of relatively small steps (to build momentum), followed by extra-long strikes towards the end of the finishing line (assisted by the momentum). Most success coaches will testify to the well-tested coaching style of *consistency over intensity*. In other words, it is easier to start with a routine that is easier and doable and then build momentum from there. Kaizen is the key to consistency and sustained effort in any worthy endeavour.

There is also the 5-minute rule[28] being used as a cognitive behavioural therapy technique for procrastination. The idea is that you aim to do an activity in 5 minutes, and if you think it is not doable, you are free to stop. 5 minutes accomplished. However, it is observed that most people do *carry on* even after 5 minutes are over. The conceptual approach here is the commencement is the hardest part, aka inertia. However, once you are in motion for 5 minutes, you will have built the momentum and overcome the inertia. The brain perceives that a 5-minute task is so doable that the decision to do it is almost effortless, and there is no overthinking. This is the brain hack to break a task or challenge into chewable doable tasks. Incidentally, there is a variant to the 5-minute rule called the 1-minute rule, by author and *happiness expert* Gretchen Rubin (2006) that stipulates that if a task can be completed in one minute or less, it should be done immediately, like washing a dish, keeping the books back to bookshelves, folding the blanket, or answering an email. The idea is that keeping all the small nagging tasks under control would make you more serene and less overwhelmed.

Still on the subject of inertia, interestingly, there is a Chinese idiom that propounds that many things are difficult in the beginning (万事起头难). In a wider sense, many things would be difficult because of unfamiliarity. Also, the force of habit[29] has not kicked in yet. However, one of the reasons for many things being *difficult* is simply because of inertia. Imagine starting a car engine on a cold winter morning is a challenge sometimes (especially for older models), but once it is properly warmed up, the mechanism becomes more fluid.

---

28 Invented by Goetz Graefe, Hewlett-Packard Lab 1987.
29 See Chapter 3 for this powerful concept.

Now, if we can harness that and switch on this underrated power of Kaizen at will, break off the inertia, and know the strategies to *sustain* the momentum, many worthy endeavours of ours will see beautiful and bountiful outcomes. Using the Newtonian formula of $F = ma$ (Force is equal to mass times acceleration) as an analogy, if you want to be a force to be reckoned with, there must be a combination of *motivation* and *action*. Indeed, it has been elegantly said that the distance between dream and reality is called action (and lots of massive actions). Linguistically, the Chinese word for *activity* is called Huodong (活動), which is made up of 2 words, life and movement. My friends, if you want to live, you must move! No wonder the medical community now has the mantra *"sitting is the new cancer or the new smoking"*, meaning a sedentary lifestyle can perniciously wreak havoc on our health and even cause illnesses such as cardiac malfunctions and cancer growth.

The global success story of *Kumon Centres*, the phenomenal self-learning Maths teaching technique from Japan, is another manifestation of Kaizen. The founder, Toru Kumon San, wanted to help his son (Takeshi san) in Maths, and in the process, created this Kumon method in Osaka, Japan, which eventually took the world by storm[30]. In its essence, students learn to do the worksheets independently from the point that they do easily, without making judgements based on age or school grade level. Once they are competent at a certain level and feel a sense of accomplishment, they move to the next level (altogether 21 levels). No skipping or shortcuts. A few takeaway messages here: everyone learns at a different pace (there is no one-size-fits-all learning speed), there is no need to compare, and incremental progress works (Kaizen). Once there is measurable progress at the pace the student can manage (no rush, and you don't feel overwhelmed), it fuels self-confidence, which then motivates the student to build the momentum of progress.

"Be not afraid of going slowly, be afraid only of standing still."
[不怕慢, 只怕站] **Chinese saying**

Speaking of momentum, the famous scientist Sir Isaac Newton has some sound advice to offer on this 3rd planet of ours too. You see, the 3 fundamental laws formulated by Sir Isaac Newton[31] resonate and reaffirm the principle contained in the spirit of Kaizen. Newton states that a body at rest stays at rest,

---

30 Over 26,000 learning centres in 55 countries!
31 *Mathematical Principles of Natural Philosophy*, by Sir Isaac Newton (1687), English edition (1728)

and a body in motion stays in motion. That's the 1st Law of motion. In fact, given its universal application on planet Earth, a motor vehicle's safety belt is made mandatory in most countries, as we don't get to negotiate with the 1st Newtonian law when the vehicle is moving at breakneck speed.

Interestingly, Newton's 1st law is also called the Law of *Inertia*. And *momentum* describes the relationship between speed, mass, and direction. The importance of momentum in Physics cannot be underestimated. In the Newtonian universe, they talk about applying force[32] to stop or move an object. As the story goes, a stationary steamtrain can be prevented from moving by a mere triangular block under the wheel, but a full-speed moving steamtrain can smash through a concrete wall. The power of momentum is illustrated in everyday life. You see, you don't get to negotiate with momentum when you drive your car at top speed without buckling up your safety belt. An interesting historical fact: When the seat belt first came into the safety of the automobile scene in the 1960s, there was a protest group against the wearing of the seatbelt, on the argument of *civil liberty,* in that it violated the right to bodily privacy and self-control. (Well, we will leave it to those protesters to *negotiate* with the Newtonian principle of momentum when their cars are at high speed.)

It's been said that the father of all actions is DECISION and that the original meaning of the word *decision* in Latin literally means to cut off all other options.[33] The other English word to capture this essence is *single-mindedness*. Powerful words. And by extension, what then is the mother of all results? It is ACTIONS and lots of it. Indeed, a true decision would generate a lot of follow-through actions, given that all other options have been literally cut off. No distraction, just laser-sharp focus, energy, and direction. Conceptually speaking, then, the father and mother of our life's destiny would be DECISIONS and ACTIONS. Where our mindset is Kaizen (to seek daily and continuous improvements) and followed by lots of actions, then incremental improvement would be our daily mantra, and embracing the mindset of ourselves being *work-in-progress* becomes second nature.

The question remains: How do we ensure that we can continuously tap and develop this beneficial Kaizen strategy, ingrain it into our mindset, and sustain it in our daily lifestyles and activities? This is where the 3rd powerful step comes in…

---

[32] F= ma. Force equals mass times acceleration.
[33] In Latin it is DECIDERE, de= off + ceadere= cut.

CHAPTER 3

HELLO HABITS, NICE TO MEET YOU, EVERY DAY!

"The chains of habit are generally too small to be felt until they are too strong to be broken."
– Samuel Johnson, an English writer, 1709-1784,
who wrote A Dictionary of the English Language.

Do you debate or remind yourself to brush your teeth in the morning or at night? Have you ever forgotten to put toothpaste when you brush your teeth? Chances are you have developed such a routine *daily and repeatedly for the umpteenth time* to the point where it is almost on autopilot. In fact, you probably would be thinking about your plan for the day or to-do list, or your mind would be wandering *whilst* you are brushing your teeth. That, my friend, is the *power* of habit. And just to illustrate my point, try brushing your teeth this week with your non-dominant hand and see how awkward it is (and for those of you who are ambidextrous in brushing your teeth, you are excused from this challenge).

In everyday understanding, habits are thoughts, activities, and actions that are *repeated* so often that they become second nature or a routine. The Chinese have a saying for this-习惯成自然(meaning the habitual practice until it became natural). The Merriam-Webster Dictionary defines a habit as a settled tendency or usual manner of behaviour. The way we understand habit, it is actually a learned behaviour that becomes reflexive over time. So, what does it have to do with mental fitness? You see, there are various kinds of habits. You have habits that are good and beneficial (like brushing your teeth, regularly hydrating yourself by drinking water, and saying thank you a lot), habits that are bad (like nail-biting, binge-watching TV series, smoking, and Facebook[34] indulgence, eating junk food) and neutral or harmless habits (like wearing one sock then one shoe, or both socks, then only the shoes, or wiping your head first after a shower). It has been said that we are all creatures of habits.

"Practice isn't the thing that you do once and you're good. It's the thing you do that makes you good."
– Malcolm Gladwell

The 2 recent names in the field of systematic study or understanding of habits are Charles Duhigg[35] and James Clear[36]. Both these brilliant authors have contributed so much to the science of developing habits. And just in case you think that habits are only *recently* being acknowledged to be important to our daily living, actually the great philosopher Aristotle observed its profound influence on human beings thousands of years ago. Here's the news flash from the famous ancient philosopher[37]: *95% of everything you do is the result of habits!* Wauzeeeee! So, the trick is, if you know *how* to nurture habits and replace bad habits with good habits, your life will be optimised to an almost effortless, pseudo-autopilot mode. In fact, phrases like *force of habit* and *old habits die hard* bear testimony to this irrefutable truth of our human nature and mental makeup. In fact, it is remarkable that Dr. Steven Covey even called his bestseller book *The Seven **Habits** of Highly Effective People*[38], and not 7 systems, or even 7 strategies.

"First, forget inspiration. Habit is more dependable. Habit will sustain you whether you're inspired or not."
– Octavia Butler[39]

One of my all-time favourite comedians is Jerry Seinfeld[40] of the sitcom *Seinfeld*, which was from NBC from 1989 to 1998. In fact, word on the street is that the iconic hanging bicycle in his apartment had influenced many viewers to take up cycling and even hang up the bike in a similar fashion. Okay, back

---

[34] Facebook changed its name to Meta in Oct 2021.
[35] Charles Duhigg on The Power of Habit (2012)
[36] James Clear on Atomic Habits (2018)
[37] Aristotle (384-322 BC)
[38] First published in 1989, in USA by Free Press. Sold more than 25 million copies.
[39] Octovia Estelle Butler, (1947-2006), famous American science fiction writer, and the 1st science fiction writer to receive the MacArthur Fellowship, a kind of "Genius grant".
[40] Born April 29, 1954, named by Comedy Central as the 12th greatest stand-up comedian of all time in 2004.

to Seinfeld, and what has he got to do with the powers of habits? You see, Jerry Seinfeld became a successful comedian earning lots of money over his TV series and royalties. A young comedian by the name of Brad Isaac wanted to learn his trade secret and got him to share it in one of those backstage encounters. And Jerry Seinfeld shared with Brad that what he needed to do was to get a huge annual 365-day calendar and display it prominently in his study area, and make sure that he crosses a big X on the day that he writes some funny jokes or ideas. And here was the key: do not leave too many blanks between the Xs. The takeaway message is to build *consistency* and turn it into a *daily* habit. In the end, daily consistency beats sporadic intensity.

"We are what we repeatedly do, excellence, then, is not an act, but a habit."
– Aristotle (384-322 BC)

Jack Canfield[41] hit the nail on its head when he said that *"Your habits will determine your future"*. Success coaches are now advocating a *strong morning routine* to kickstart the day. This strong morning routine has been observed in many accomplished leaders, and the specific routine (be it meditation, juicing, reading, journaling, or exercising) is practised daily until they are performed almost on autopilot. No time is wasted in the morning decision-making process. One of the sound reasons for such a repeated routine is to minimise what we call decision fatigue or even decision paralysis. The brain takes energy to process the options and to make a decision or even to stall a decision. Good habits take the heat off the brain, giving the brain more energy to focus on more arduous, challenging, or even creative tasks.

In fact, there was a jam experiment done in 2000 jointly by Columbia and Stanford Universities[42] where 24 different kinds of jam were offered in a food market on certain days, and 6 different types of jams were offered on other days. The marketing hypothesis for consumer behaviour is if they increase the varieties to 24 different jams compared to just 6 types, the sales should increase because you are giving the consumers more choices, right? The result? The sales dropped significantly for the 24 varieties' days. It turned out that decision paralysis and decision fatigue overwhelmed the customers, and they decided *not to commit* to buying the jam in the case of 24 jams' varieties, as compared to the 6 jams' varieties. That's called the *paradox of choice*.[43]

---

41 American author, motivational speaker and co-author of the "Chicken Soup for the Soul" series.

42 By Psychologists Sheena Ivengar (Columbia University) and Mark Lepper (Stanford University)

43 *Baskins Robbins's* 31 flavours may be another category altogether, as resistance to ice-cream is futile, especially with the tag line of one flavor a day for a month from the world largest ice cream store (>8,000 stores worldwide).

The good news is—when we know and understand the science of habits and learn to tap into the proper cue and reinforcement techniques, and once the habits (good ones of course) are ingrained into our daily routines, then decision paralysis, decision fatigue, and the paradox of choice would be minimised, enabling our brain to focus on deep work or creative tasks which require lots of brain juice. Again, the brain becomes *indistractible*.

The other observation to make is that we invariably develop habits either mindlessly or mindfully. A lot has been written on the benefits of living our lives mindfully or intentionally, especially in this 24/7 social media numbing culture. Also, we will be influenced by the environment, peer pressure, personal preference and even the self-gratification pull. However, as Dr. Steven Covey put it so eloquently, *We are not products of our circumstances, but the products of our decisions.* That said, the powerful effect of habits is that they subconsciously bypass or hijack our decision-making mechanism in so many ways. The trick is to *observe* ourselves and understand how these habits have been formed over the weeks, months, and even years. Do an honest self-audit of your various habits. And given that we are all a bundle of our daily habits, it is vital to continuously do a *decluttering* of bad habits and *replace* them with good ones. Kaizen!

Embracing progressive change (Kaizen) and knowing that we *can* change for the better (growth mindset) are crucial precursors to *replacing* bad habits with good habits. Change is difficult at times, and our ingrained force of habits will fight it. As mentioned earlier, try brushing your teeth with your non-dominant hand (or sign your usual signature with your non-dominant hand), you will appreciate how hard it can be. However, constancy of purpose, tiny steps (aka doable steps), celebrating mini victories, cue sequencing, positive and immediate reinforcement, and following through with *repeated* practice would then mould the activity into a routine, and the next thing you know, the habit is formed. In many synergistic ways, mindset, Kaizen, and good habits are *powerful allies* for optimising our daily lives.

Amazing strategies for the brain. The next question is: Where does that leave our body, and how does it benefit from the toughening of the brain?

CHAPTER 4

BODY-MIND DISCONNECT?

The popular running shoes that you see in sports shops, *ASICS* (アシックス, *Ashikkusu*), do you know that it is an acronym? It stands for *"Sound mind in a sound body"*, which in Latin is *anima sana in corpore sano*. The famous brand belongs to a huge Japanese corporation, which produces sports equipment designed for a wide range of sports. In fact, their running shoes have often been ranked among the top performance footwear in the world. We will explore the powerful tagline encapsulated by ASICS in this chapter.

Previously, it was thought that there was no real connection (or even communication) between the mind and the body. In fact, there is a school of thought that believes that the body exists purely to house the brain and serves the purpose of protecting and sustaining the brain. Period. Thomas Edison took the view that the chief function of the body is to carry the brain around. However, the scientific community is waking up to the exciting psychosomatic discoveries that have been mind-blowing, and that in many ways, the brain and the body are in *constant 2-way superhighway communication* with each other. The exciting field of hypnosis and hypnotherapy also bears testimony to the power of brain-body communication.[44]

There is also the brain-heart coherence concept which proposes that the brain and heart work in concert, creating a harmonious physiological state that enhances our overall well-being. This idea is rooted in the understanding

---

[44] An American teen rehabilitation center that was founded with the mission to provide teens and their families with the highest quality care and treatment for trauma, mental health issues, eating disorders, and substance abuse.

that the brain and heart are in seamless, complex communication, influencing each other's functions. Through this bidirectional communication, the heart sends signals to the brain that can affect emotional and cognitive processes. Research[45] has shown that when the heart's rhythm is coherent, it sends positive signals to the brain, promoting a state of mental clarity, emotional stability, and optimal physical functioning. The result could be quantitatively measured. Conversely, when we are stressed or depressed, our physical health will be impacted by the pernicious effect of incoherence.

Achieving brain-heart coherence involves practices that synchronise the rhythms of these 2 vital organs. Techniques such as deep breathing, meditation, and mindfulness can help foster this coherence. When we focus on positive emotions like gratitude, compassion, and love, our heart rhythm becomes more orderly and coherent. This coherent heart rhythm, in turn, enhances the brain's ability to process information, make decisions, and maintain emotional balance. The state of coherence is not only beneficial for our mental fitness but also supports physical health by reducing stress, lowering blood pressure, and improving the immune response.

The implications of brain-heart coherence extend to various aspects of life, including personal well-being, professional performance, and interpersonal relationships. People who regularly practice techniques to achieve coherence often report higher levels of resilience, improved focus, and better stress management. Moreover, the positive emotional state associated with coherence can lead to more harmonious social interactions and a greater sense of connectedness with others. In essence, brain-heart coherence is a powerful tool for cultivating a balanced, healthy, and fulfilling life, highlighting the profound interconnection between the brain and the heart, as well as our emotional and physical states.

The gut-brain connection is another explosive scientific discovery that scientists are making fantastic inroads. As it turns out, we each have about 37-39 trillion bacteria[46] in our gut (more than the stars in the sky!) and gut bacteria have strong communication with the brain. Specifically, we each

---

[45] Dynamic correlations between heart and brain rhythm during Autogenic meditation. (2013) Seoul, Korea.

[46] Don't worry about the colossal number, as in terms of weight ratio, it is only 0.3% of our overall body weight.

have a gut-brain axis (GBA), which consists of bidirectional communication between the central and the enteric nervous system, linking emotional and cognitive centres of the brain with peripheral intestinal functions. In fact, it has been observed in lab research in animals that changes in the gut microbiome and inflammation in the gut can directly affect the brain and cause symptoms that resemble Parkinson's disease, autism, anxiety, and even depression. The bottom line—they are all *connected*. It is time that we learn to see our body and brain/mind as a *unified* whole.

The seminal research done by Dr. Wendy Suzuki[47] on how we *can* boost our brain's health through aerobic activities (or any sustained physical activity) reached its full glory when in a TED Talk[48], the energetic Dr. Suzuki even got the entire audience to stand up and do the aerobic activity on the spot to prove her super enthusiastic point. The takeaway message is this: *Regularly* engage in about 30 minutes of brisk walking, Shirin-Yoko hike, cycling, swimming or any other aerobic activities that can hyper-oxygenate your brain via the pumping of the heart, about 5 times a week. Dr. Wendy Suzuki calls it a "bubble bath for the brain". We have also talked about the Chinese word for activity in Chapter 2 on movement, that if you want to live, you really got to move— consistently. Indeed, one of the key common denominators from the study of the 5 Blue Zones in the world[49] (where they have the highest concentration of centenarians) is that the inhabitants are invariably on the move, every day.

Now, in our body, we have haemoglobin, which is red blood cells (iron-containing protein), that transport oxygen to the various tissues throughout our bodies. They are super important; they ensure that our vital organs are well-oxygenated. A sedentary lifestyle means not much movement and distribution for the oxygen carriers, and conversely, an active moving body helps to mobilise the haemoglobin in their distribution network in the circulatory system. The following paragraph further explains *why* movement is so crucial to our body's oxygenation.

For those of you who are more science-based in your thinking, there are 2 forces at work for molecules: cohesive force and adhesive force. Cohesive

---

[47] *Happy Brain, Happy Life* (2015) By Dr Wendy Suzuki (Neuroscientist)
[48] Nov 2017, in New Orleans (Louisiana), 13 million plus views.
[49] Okinawa island (Japan), Sardina (Italy), Loma Linda (California), Ikaria (Greece) & Nicoya (Costa Rica).

force is when like molecules stick together, and adhesive force is when different molecules stick together. I have personally seen via an electron microscope how a droplet of blood (i.e., lots and lots of haemoglobin) behaves between 2 slices of holding glasses. You will see that when the 2 glasses that clamp the blood droplet are at rest (no agitation or movement), the haemoglobin would come together in a lump. That's the cohesive force at play. However, just a gentle tap on the top of the glass (asserting a light pressure between the 2 pieces of holding glasses), you would observe that the red blood cells would be spread out. And we know that, the red blood cells would increase their overall surface area and their distribution outreach in a spread-out pattern. The key takeaway message is that movement (aka exercise) helps to minimise the cohesive force among the oxygen carriers, i.e., haemoglobin and will help to make the circulatory system more efficient. In short, a sedentary lifestyle equals lethargy, and an active lifestyle equals vibrancy.

The other system in our amazing body to highlight is the lymphatic system. Not as popular as the circulatory system, but it plays an important role in our body. You see, the lymphatic system is instrumental in getting rid of toxins and cellular waste from our bodies and also in transporting lymph (the fluid that carries the white blood cells) throughout the body. In this sense, it is part of the circulatory system and immune system. Here's the thing to remember, unlike the circulatory system (which is assisted by the heart to pump the red blood cells for circulatory motion), the lymphatic system cannot move until moved upon, meaning an active lifestyle. Here's another jaw-dropping fun fact quiz about our magnificent body: if you were to join all the ventricles, veins, and arteries in your body end-to-end, guess how loooooong it would be? 10 metres? 10 km? 50 km? Please see the footnote for the astounding answer![50] And that's more than twice the circumference of the Earth! Now you have a compelling and colossal reason to move your body regularly.

Of course, other factors would also clog the lymphatic system (imagine the buildup of toxins in your body), such as lack of sleep, dehydration, stress, or infection. However, lack of movement has an immediate negative impact on the efficiency of our lymphatic system. On this score, the rebounder/trampoline is a superb exercise device to jump-start our lymphatic system. This has to do with anti-gravity motion, which is what the lymphatic system needs. Don't worry. If you don't have a rebounder/trampoline, then skipping rope, aerobics,

---

50 About 97,000km, I-kid-you-not. ☺

running, hiking, brisk walking, and swimming are wonderful exercises for the lymphatic system. Your body and your brain will thank you for such self-care.

Also, if you don't move, your muscles will eventually shrink and waste. The medical term *Sarcopenia*[51] describes the syndrome characterised by progressive and generalised loss of skeletal muscle mass and strength, and the shrinking starts in our 30s to 40s. The primary treatment for Sarcopenia is exercise, especially resistance training or strength training. Indeed, there is a direct correlation between physical inactivity and loss of muscle mass and strength. The catchphrase, *If you don't use it, you will lose it*, is so true for our muscles. And by extension, if you don't exercise, your muscles will eventually degenerate, and with less exercise, the brain gets less oxygen, which means the brain cannot function at its optimal level. You become less productive in your thinking, your mood is not upbeat, and your BMI goes south, which in turn causes you to be even more lethargic, and demotivates you from getting out of the comfy sofa. This *is* the vicious cycle of degenerative health, both mental and physical.

The hunger drive is another marvellous manifestation of the mind-body connection. As we all know, we get our nutrients from food, and food enters our body principally via our mouth, where mastication (our teeth chewing and crushing the food) and saliva initiate the process of breaking down the food into smaller digestible portions. It then passes down via the oesophagus to the stomach to be further processed by the strong acid and then to the small intestines for the nutrients to be extracted and assimilated in our daily mental and bodily functions. The *leftovers* are then passed down to the big intestine to be excreted in due course. That is the summarised version of our marvellous digestive system. [Here's an out-of-the-box (or out-of-body) perspective of the food intake in our body: that the food or liquid is technically not yet in our body system until they are *assimilated* via the epidemic layers within the digestive tract.]

Here's the evolutionary insight: Eating is so important (think survival) that the nerve cells of appetite are located in the hypothalamus region of the brain. Speaking about eating, it's been said that good nutrition will prevent 95% of all diseases. Truth be told, we should all eat like our lives depend on it, because it does! And interestingly, the brain takes about 20-30% of

---

[51] Originates from the Greek words "sarx" which flesh, and "penia" which means poverty. First proposed by IH Rosenberg in 1989.

the nutrients consumed by us daily. Now, many types of diets have been popularised over the years, from vegetarian, pescatarian, carnivore, keto, pure fruits, omnivore, Atkins diet to South Beach diet (from Miami, USA), veganism, and Mediterranean diet. It can be confusing to some, and there is no one-size-fits-all diet. There is also the Western diet vs Asian diet dichotomy and exotic cuisine ranging from Indian, Japanese, and Thai to Italian culinary styles. Explore them by all means; just remember that we each have one body to take care of, and it's the only one that we have. Nutritionally speaking, the guy who grew up and is living in Alaska would not benefit from the daily diet of the guy who grew up and lives in the Sahara desert, and vice versa. I used to attend a city gym in Kuala Lumpur after my office hours when I started working after university, and I remember a muscular-looking gym instructor by the name of Michael. He told me that *if I don't take care of my body, nobody else will*. That was an epiphany moment for me.

The brain has been called the most amazing and mystifying evolved organ, confounding scientists, and how it communicates with the body's physiology is truly a wonder beyond words—from the ability to put the body on instant alert in imminent danger to pumping out the hunger trigger when the glycaemic level is low, and to even *unload* the stress to various parts of the body to share the load. The nutrients that we feed our body naturally include nutrients to our brains. The good science and research from nutritionists have highlighted the benefits of certain high-antioxidant superfoods that are beneficial to our body, especially our gut, heart and also our brains, such as salmon, blueberries, chia seeds, flax seeds, avocado, spinach, broccoli, walnuts, oats, yoghurt, fermented cabbage, green tea, cocoa, coconut, and many more with all their cancer-fighting abilities and nutrient-rich contents. In fact, eating well is a form of self-care that should not be taken for granted. The Kaizen technique here is to gradually increase our daily intake of all these superfoods and to also gradually decrease or replace junk food and processed food with these superfoods, be it our 3 daily meals or even as snacks. Bottom line: Good nutritional habits will serve us well in optimal living and sustain us in our old age.

Given that the brain is constantly communicating with the body, the question then to ask is this: What is your mind telling your body? Here's the thing, our body will believe what our mind tells it. The news flash is this: The conversation that you have with yourself (self-talk) has a profound impact on your mental and physical well-being. The next chapter explores this powerful and yet overlooked phenomenon.

CHAPTER 5

YOU ARE TALKING TO YOURSELF?

How many thoughts do we have in a single day? 20? 100? 1000? According to research findings, we can have an average of 12,000 to 80,000 thoughts a day! That's an average of 500 to 3,300 thoughts per hour, assuming you are fully awake 24 hours. Deduct 8 hours for sleep, that's 750 to 5,000 thoughts per hour daily. No wonder we are so exhausted mentally many times! That is the silent power of SELF-TALK. It can be beneficial to our mind, or it can cause havoc. Here's the news flash: The way you talk to yourself creates *your* reality.

"Life is what you dwell on. If you dwell on the negative, life is negative. If you dwell on the positive, life is positive."
– Terry Orlick, Canadian sports psychologist.

So, the question is, how exactly do we have an empowering and positive conversation with ourselves? The first step is self-awareness. Be mindful when you hear yourself having an internal conversation. If we learn to observe and monitor our self-talk, we *can* gradually recalibrate many of the conversations throughout the day (think Kaizen) to jettison all the toxicity and bring back the calm and tranquillity to our brain's ethos. The following are some of the brain hacks or mindset shifts to regain optimal inner conversation:

1. Any thought or conversation that is negative or destructive in content, recognise it and learn to reframe it, for example, by using the glass-half-

full mindset. Learn to see the good in the scenario. And if you still can't, focus on *Wabi-Sabi*[52], the acceptance process can be therapeutic.

A simple illustration: Say you are walking along the sidewalk and ... see your friend walking on the other side of the road in the opposite direction. You wave to him or her. But he or she does not wave back. A few self-talk options pop up in your mind:

A. He/she did not see me;

B. He/she did not see me because he/she was preoccupied with thoughts;

C. He/she saw me but is ignoring me because he/she is anti-social;

D. He/she saw me but is ignoring me because he/she is having an unresolved issue and didn't feel like being sociable;

E. He/she saw me but is ignoring me because he/she has an unresolved issue *with me* and doesn't feel like being sociable;

F. He/she is ignoring me because he/she is being rude to me;

G. He/she is deliberately ignoring me because he/she doesn't like me;

H. He/she is avoiding me because he/she does not want to be my friend.

(I reckon some of us even get stressed out going through the various options in our heads…)

As you will observe, the further down the options go, the more stressful, harmful, or even more toxic the thought process becomes. The fact of the matter is that we are conjecturing or speculating on the other person's lack of response. If we develop the *habit* of giving the friend the *benefit of the doubt* and learn to see the glass half-full, we will then learn to have less toxic conjecture against our friend. (And even in the unpleasant-case scenario, should the friend want to become anti-social or ignore or dislike us, it is okay, just don't overthink it. Chapter 11 on the 3 Circles talks more about how to handle such a scenario.)

"Don't be a victim of negative self-talk, remember you are listening."
– Bob Proctor.

2. Recognise that any thought process remains a thought functionally. Where it is a reflection of a past event, then 2 clear options exist. If it is a wonderful and pleasant experience, be grateful for it. If it was a painful

---

[52] See Chapter 10 on this discussion.

or destructive event, an error in judgement, or a lapse in judgement, ask yourself, what can I *learn* from it, and move on. In case of a future event, if it is a wonderful or pleasant event then go ahead, plan, or organise your to-do list, etc. If it is a challenging or unpleasant event, then be careful in the scenario building. By all means, create the worst-case scenario and ask if you can handle it. Once you are able to do this, then *everything else* that transpires would literally be an improvement, as you are mentally prepared for the worst, so to speak. See also the insightful observation by Mark Twain[53] on this issue:

"I am an old man and have known a great many troubles, but most of them never happened."

3. If you are having a thought process, learn to have the habit of *mental closure* on that thought. If you can't, then learn to mentally KIV it, with a conscious interim mental closure too. Don't leave a thought *hanging* inside your head without a mental closure. What do I mean by mental closure? Let me use our desktop computer to illustrate. When we work on any assignment or project, we open up a lot of windows on our computer screen, create tabs for them, and cross-reference the various tabs in our assignment or project. And then we notice that the computer processing slows down considerably after a while. We are then advised by our IT-savvy colleague to close the unused tabs and not to have too many tabs opened, as it would slow down the processing speed. It is good to declutter the computer in this regard. It's the same with our thought *tabs*. You see, our brain is somewhat like our computer; it can have a lot of mental tabs (many thoughts) to be opened, worked on, KIVed, and to be continued later. It is not an issue if it is just a few mental tabs. Mental stress comes when it accumulates to the hundreds or more in an individual; that's when we can't focus at will, get stressed out, and become short-fused and snap easily.

4. So, how exactly do you achieve this *mental closure*? A thought can be just a thought. I want to eat an apple. That's a thought. Should I eat an apple or an orange? That's a simple dialogue requiring a simple decision. But *conversational* self-talk can be extensive or even complex by many folds, be it a relationship matter, commercial venture decision, conflict resolution options, or reflecting on a misunderstanding. That self-talk

---

[53] Attributed by Reader's Digest, April 1934.

can be wonderful, self-assuring, noisy, confusing, hypothetical, scenario-building, insightful, an epiphany moment, a worst-case-scenario building, a lightbulb moment, and on and on. And sometimes it is not concluded or unresolved, it remains a hanging thought or a lingering thought. Too many of those and the mind gets stressed, weary, or drained. In other words, a noisy mind or as they say, "too many monkeys" in the mind. Mindlessness.

5. With such noises and opened *tabs*, the ability to stay focused on a single task becomes a challenge. The trick is to learn to mindfully *close* or at least *minimise* them in your mental catalogue. Self-talk like "I can't resolve it yet, but I will come back to it later when I am more refreshed"; "It's okay, I can't control that event or person—I will accept it with *Wabi-sabi*[54]"; "What is the half-full glass here?" or "How does that relate to my 3 eulogies[55]?" "Would this matter in 5 years' time?" "Let's get back to my Circle of Control…" "Perspective here—did anybody die?" will help to close or minimise the mental tabs, giving your mind more decluttered space to focus on the task at hand or be more present in your engagement with surrounding or friends or loved ones.

"Don't get upset with your negative self-talk. Just observe it without judgement, like birds flying by and it will pass."
– Lolita Guarin

More than 30 years ago, Dr. Pamela E Butler[56], in her seminal book on self-talk entitled *Talking to Yourself- Learning the Language of Self-Affirmation*[57], talked about how negative thoughts and emotions produce negative changes in the body, but also that there is a proximate relationship between overcoming depression and regaining health. In fact, scientists have discovered that high-grade gliomas—the most fatal type of brain tumour—increase in size by hijacking the process of creating thoughts. Specifically, they hijack a process called myelination, which creates a protective layer around nerve fibres, allowing them to carry thoughts more quickly. The takeaway message is that your thoughts *can* fuel brain tumours [58]. A caveat, given that the research was

---

[54] See Chapter 10 on this amazing topic.
[55] See Chapter 11 on this confounding and empowering concept.
[56] Clinical Psychologist based in California.
[57] Revised edition (1991) Published by HarperSanFancisco
[58] Stanford University, 2015, Michelle Monje

done on mice, it remains a *theoretical* possibility that thoughts might influence tumour growth in humans (the experiment used optogenetic stimulation, which is a highly artificial way of increasing brain activity like jump-starting millions of neurons all at once).

"There is nothing good or bad, but thinking makes it so."
Act 2, Scene 2, Hamlet, Shakespeare

Every day, make a conscious effort to be curious and intentionally observe your daily internal conversation (from a 3rd party perspective). There is an old fable of a Red-Indian chief telling his grandson the story of the white wolf and the black wolf where every day the white wolf and the black wolf fight with each other, and here's the thing—they are a figurative expression, and both live inside each of us. The grandson, being the usual inquisitive one, swallowed his saliva, then asked his grandpa, "So, who usually wins?" The grandpa took a deep inhalation of his good ol' pipe, puffed, and then looked lovingly at his grandson, and said: *"The one you feed, of course!"*

Incorporate the power of mindset into the arena of self-talk; it is amazing how we can transform our attitude and approach to living by reframing the words we use to talk to ourselves. Just take the simple *I can't* whenever it pops up in your internal conversation and replace it with *not yet*. Our mindset will then move from a limiting mindset to a *possibilities* mindset. Another 2 empowering words that can turbo-charge your mindset in self-talk are *Why not?*, instead of *cannot*. George Bernard Shaw summed it up well in this quote: *"You see things and you say Why?; But I dream things that never were and I say, Why not?"*. Such simple linguistic recalibration (aka mindset change) can unleash the true potential of our brain and spice up our daily Kaizen. Even the syntax of these 2 words—one and day—will move the goalpost or energise you into massive action: *"One Day or Day One, you decide."*

"For true success, ask yourself these 4 questions:

Why? Why not? Why not me? Why not now?"
– James Allen

In the end, mindfully guard your internal dialogue. The elephant in the room here is that these internal self-talks are *as real as reality* for many of us, and yet not much attention is given to it, precisely because it is *completely silent* to the person sitting next to you. Awareness is the beginning of self-discovery and a constructive path to pruning our internal conversation. There is an SOS technique to minimise or arrest any negative self-talk that wants to dominate our mind: Consciously tell yourself to **STOP** to give the opportunity to arrest the negative thought, interrupt the thought cycle (or replace it with a positive half-glass full thought), mindfully **OBSERVE** what you are actually saying to yourself and how it is making you feel, and **SHIFT** your thought process to a more constructive and cheerful cognitive endeavour.

Now, let us move the internal dialogue to the arena of gratification next…

CHAPTER 6

DELAYED GRATIFICATION

The problem with the prevailing trend and culture of our present society is *instant* gratification with enabling technologies that can give us instant noodles, instant answers by the click of the *enter* button, and the ability to binge-show TV series (instead of waiting for one episode per week), we have become rather impatient with the concept of waiting, and a few seconds delay in any video download becomes *annoying* (not to worry, 5G is on the way…). So, what has delayed gratification got to do with mental fitness?

Well, it has to do with impulse and self-control. For those of you who have not heard of the famous Marshmallow experiment, it was conducted by an Austrian-born American psychologist Walter Mischel, a Stanford University professor, way back in 1972. Essentially, a child was offered a choice of one marshmallow for an immediate reward or 2 marshmallows if he or she waited for a while. (I suppose American kids LOVE marshmallows. If your local culture is more into lollipops or doughnuts, you may mentally substitute the reward/sweetener here.) Instinct and the impulse for immediate gratification favour the one marshmallow and the now-here immediate enjoyment. On the other hand, with self-control and deliberate patience, the child is later rewarded with *one extra* marshmallow. Remarkably, the follow-up study and subsequent studies discovered that the children who were patient enough to wait for the 2 marshmallows tend to do better in life in terms of achievements and handling challenges.

Actually, Professor Walter Mischel never expected the extensive effect and correlation his marshmallow experiment has on a child's ability to cope in later life. However, as peer review and follow-up studies show, there is a meaningful correlation between the ability to control one's impulse and the cultivation of patience for a more bountiful outcome. In fact, Professor Walter Mischel went on to write a book in 2014 about the Marshmallow experiment, which he aptly titled *THE MARSHMALLOW TEST - Why Self-control is the Engine of Success*, and the Mindset Guru, Dr. Carol Dweck, called this book "An amazing, eye-opening, transformative, riveting, book from one of the greatest psychologists of our time." Since the famous Marshmallow experiment, there has been lots of follow-up research on self-control and willpower—whether it is prewired or whether it can be learned. Well, the good news from Professor Walter Mischel is that the ability to delay immediate gratification is an acquirable cognitive skill.

In the ancient Chinese idiom, there is a famous idiom, *"bitterness first, sweetness later"* (先苦後甜), which espouses the concept of suffering/bitterness first, then only sweetness later. The often-told fable related by my mum is that of the wise emperor who eats the sugar cane, in that he would eat the not-so-sweet portion first and then finish off with the sweet portion (Not to worry, I won't ask you how you eat your slice of pizza). There is wisdom in that, which resonates with the concept of delayed gratification. Indeed, nurtured discipline is a function of self-control, and conversely, lack of focus tends to be associated with impulsive behaviour.

Even in finance and budgeting, instant gratification has a negative impact on savings and sound budgeting, especially when *impulse* buying feeds on retail therapy (the super-easy 24-hour access to online shopping apps do not help). On the other hand, delayed gratification has allowed a person to withhold unnecessary spending, resulting in the compounded growth of savings, enabling prudent investment, which in turn will help buffer for financial emergencies and *rainy days*", so to speak. Truth be told, financial stress caused by a lack of proper budgeting can wear down the brain.

The 15th-century French philosopher, Michael de Montaigne, has even attested as follows: *I conceive that pleasures are to be avoided if greater pains be the consequence, and pains be coveted that will terminate in greater pleasures*. Wise observation indeed, and another variant and endorsement of delayed gratification. In fact, I dare say it is the common mantra of many super-athletes. Remember the tagline often heard in gyms—no pain, no gain?

One of the most famous psychiatrists, Dr. M Scott Peck, who wrote the bestselling book *The Road Less Travelled*[59], has this to say about delayed gratification:

"Delaying gratification is a process of scheduling the pain and pleasure of life in such a way as to enhance the pleasure by meeting and experiencing the pain first and getting it over with. It is the only decent way to live."

What an insightful observation. In fact, in his bestselling book, *The Road Less Travelled*, Dr. Scott Peck analysed the concept of discipline as the foundation for emotional, spiritual, and psychological healthy living. By way of refresher, the ability to tap on the 3M[60], which then hone our Kaizen into a habit, will serve us well here in developing the discipline and self-control of saying no to impulsive buying, instant gratification and focusing on delayed gratification. This invariably leads to greater rewards physiologically (no weight gain issue), psychologically (increased self-worth with better self-control), and even financially (superior budgeting). It is all interconnected and mutually reinforcing.

On the same theme, the Canadian motivational speaker Brian Tracy puts it very well:

"The ability to discipline yourself to delay gratification in the short term in order to enjoy greater rewards in the long term is the indispensable prerequisite for success."

---

[59] Published in 1978, and listed by the Guinness Book of World Records as the title with the longest life on the paper-back best-seller list.
[60] See Chapter 2.

The other Canadian professor of psychology, Jordan Brent Peterson[61], also endorses this profound concept: "The successful among us delay gratification. The successful among us bargain with the future."

The other elephant in the room to tackle is the barrage of advertising lures (aka temptations) to get us to buy-buy-buy materials or stuff to *complete* our lifestyles. This is where delayed gratification is most useful—in cultivating the ability to say no to impulse buying and to mindfully manage a responsible budgeting system. Self-control in this area is not to be underrated as it has the power to create a confident personality on one end and, on the other extreme, wreak lives and families with its absence. In the end, a person with nurtured self-control is invariably well poised, centred, and able to focus at will and tends to lead a more balanced life. In contrast, a person without self-control is easily distracted, has bad habits (like drinking, smoking, or unhealthy eating), has no sense of budgeting, and tends to have health issues too. This is where the concept of delayed gratification needs to be nurtured from a young age and continuously pruned to serve a more balanced, productive, and happy life.

Interrelated to the impulsive vs deliberated response is the mindless vs mindful dynamics. When one habitually and instinctively *reacts* to pleasures, temptations, and immediate gratifications (e.g. watch TV/Netflix now, can study later), mindlessness rules the day. However, in a mindfulness approach, the student would learn the art of *pause* to allow the brain to properly process the options before responding with a congruent decision. Study first, enjoy TV/Netflix/Prime/Amazon later is then executed as the optimal sequence. The fine art of differentiating reacting from responding takes time, especially in our fast-paced go-go-go digital culture. This is where mindfulness has been espoused to be the mindset to have, not just helping us to make more deliberate and better-informed decisions but also precisely because we are mindful, we are more present, and our sense of appreciation of events and things gets on a more heightened sense.

In many ways, social media like *TikTok* and *Instagram* understand how our brain works (read: instant gratification) and use short, catchy, relevant videos to literally *arrest* our attention. Apparently, it's been said that the attention span of the new generation is now akin to that of a goldfish.

---

[61] Check out his best-seller: "The 12 rules for Life: An Antidote for Chaos" (2018)

Paradoxically, however, mindless hours are locked in these entertaining videos. This is why self-help books on focus and its impact on deep work are God-sends and are the antidote to the ubiquitous culture of instant gratification. Don't get me wrong. TikTok or a similar social media platform, used intentionally, can be a wonderful educational or even a search tool. The problem is our mind gets easily distracted by the myriads of super-interesting and captivating videos being pushed to us.

Now, some readers may get confused about the messages in this chapter, as if we need to postpone pleasures and suffer at the present moment—so as to earn the pleasures later on. In such a mindset, it can be misconstrued that happiness becomes a postponed event and that we have not *earned* the right to be happy yet. There is a clear conceptual difference between rewards and pleasures on one hand and the state of happiness on the other hand. Chapter 8 delves more in-depth into the relationship and sequencing between happiness and success. For our present purpose, we just need to distinguish the difference between pleasures and being happy. To begin with, many long-term gains take effort and time. Does that, therefore, mean we are not to be happy, or worse, we should not be happy yet? Absolutely not. Happiness is a state of mind, and pleasures are physiological and psychological enjoyments in so many ways. Happiness has many times been linked to material pleasures. However, happiness is not wholly dependent on physical or sensual pleasures. Helping some poor kids in their studies or giving a hand to paint an orphanage are altruistic activities that can also generate oxytocin and a feeling of well-being, a sense of contribution. It is not selfish but rather selfless. That is happiness too.

Bottom line: Any worthwhile endeavour takes time, and the sense of achievement and jubilation comes upon the completion of the task or activity. Kick back and relish the accomplishment. Meanwhile, Kaizen on the process, enjoy the journey and be happy.

CHAPTER 7

IN THE BEGINNING, THE END MATTERS

The story goes like this: Once, an uncle visited his 3 favourite nephews in a snowy winter. He invited all 3 of them to the white snowy field to play. He then planted a visible long pole at one end of the white snowy field and got the 3 boys to gather at the other end of the field. As excitable young boys, they were all curious about the details of the game or test that their uncle was going to give them. The uncle told them that the game was rather simple; they were to take turns walking across the field to reach the pole, and whoever walked the *straightest* line would win the contest. The eldest went first. He thought to himself, if I put one foot in *perfect* alignment with the other foot in my forward step, I would eventually reach the pole, hopefully with a straight line. So, he did that. The next boy then figured that if he just mirrored or copied my elder brother, he should be able to walk a straight line and reach the pole. The youngest nephew said to himself, the pole is my *focal point*; I just need to keep looking at the pole and walk straight in its direction; I should be able to walk a straight line. No prize for guessing which of the nephews won the contest.

The takeaway message is this: In any worthy endeavour, until and unless you have the end game clearly in sight, your journey would invariably be swayed or even off-track, given that the so-called lighthouse bearing is simply not there to guide you. Now if we are to extend it to the larger game called LIFE, the question to ask is: What *kind* of life do I want to live? That's a LOAD of questions, bordering on the meaning of life, and the philosophy of our existence, existentialist debate, bla-bla-bla; which is why most of us don't bother or would avoid the issue itself. In this regard, I am immensely grateful to Dr. Stephen R Covey's seminal work on living an *effective* life via his signature book entitled *The 7 Habits of Highly Effective People*[62], which is one of my all-time favourite self-improvement books.

Specifically, habit no 2 from Dr. Covey's book talks about beginning with the end in mind. It is essentially the visualisation in your mind of what you cannot presently see with your eyes. The relevant principle is that all things are created twice. There is the mental (first) creation, then followed by a physical (second) creation. The rule of engagement is that the physical creation *follows* the mental, just like a building follows a blueprint or a schematic design. The thing to emphasise here is that if you don't make a conscious effort to conceptualise or internalise who you are and what you want in life, then by default, you empower other people and circumstances to shape you and your life. In a sense, it is about connecting with your true uniqueness and then defining the personal, moral, and ethical guidelines through which you can most optimally express your life.

So, how exactly do we execute the visualisation process to create the compelling blueprint or the True North principles of our lives? For this, Dr. Covey's suggestion is gripping and thought-provoking, and it will galvanise your mind to grapple with the urgency of the end questions. So, here goes: Sit in a comfortable place, with zero distraction (yes, off your hand-phone), and close your eyes. Now, imagine you are driving alone one cool evening to attend a funeral. Upon arrival, you see a crowd or a congregation gathering. You see people seated in the chairs provided. You then walk respectfully towards the casket to pay your last respects. With the top of the casket open, you view the face of the deceased. Peaceful and calm is how you would describe the facial makeup of that deceased. Then, it dawns upon you that, actually, it is *you* in the casket! You are attending your own funeral. Yikes! Excuse the morbid scenario building, but stay with me for the *raison d'être* of the imagined funeral.

With that jolted realisation, you then decide to sit quietly at one of the empty chairs at the front of the congregation. The funeral director or coordinator then announced that there would be 3 eulogies to be shared that evening. The first one would be one of your family members (could be your parent, spouse, or

---

[62] Published 15th August 1989.

child), the second would be from your work colleague or working partner, and the third would be from a fellow friend or worker from your social group or interest group. Now, of course, you have no idea whatsoever (for now) about what they are going to say at your funeral. Here's the epiphany moment—what you want or desire the 3 eulogies to be shared is exactly how you are going to live your life, day by day, week by week, month by month, and year by year.

So, in the upshot, to clearly conceptualise with the end in mind, start drafting the 3 eulogies in your mind or your personal journal. The more details, the better. Make sure that you are brutally and candidly honest with your inner thoughts and self-dialogue. The 3 eulogies are conceptually the tall guiding pole at the other end of the white snowy field. Burn it into your DNA or your subconsciousness. These are the 3 blueprints for your daily directions, be it attitude, emotions, decisions, responses, social interactions or engagements, and even goal setting. The other reason why some of us live such a dispersed life rather than a focused life is that we are unfortunately driven or drawn to the tall poles of other people around us, and we either subconsciously or in a multitasking manoeuvre move or disperse towards that direction(s) too. It is then the case of us living or copying other people's dreams and goals, rather than our true authentic goals and eulogies. Note: We are all uniquely and individually made. Don't believe it? Go look for someone with the *exact* thumbprint as you. Epiphany moment.

The *clearer* the eulogies are, the better your decision-making process will be every day. Indeed, it would be the lighthouse or the True North compass that will continue to calibrate (and recalibrate) your life journey. It need not be done in one go and can be a mindful and respectful work-in-progress. (Indeed, in many ways, our lives are work-in-progress). *Life tip: Life is a gift, and every day is another opportunity to Kaizen your 3 eulogies, 1% at a time.* And if you are familiar with *Mission Statement*, a concept popularised by Dr. Stephen Covey, you can even craft your Mission Statement in line with the essence of your 3 eulogies.

Incidentally, there is a variant of a traditional funeral called a living funeral (or a pre-funeral). It is usually held by a person who knows that death is imminent (be it terminal illness or old age). The funeral is then conducted in honour of him or her for intimate sharing, articulation of appreciations (pre-eulogies?), acknowledgement of the person's contributions, and closure. The desire for such a living funeral is that the person dying will get to hear those sentimental and appreciative things while he or she is still alive. There are controversies surrounding a living funeral, ranging from the classical view that funerals are meant to honour the dead and that oftentimes a living funeral becomes egocentric. However, for our purpose, the imagined visit to our own funeral is to invoke the certainty and inevitability of death to recognise our finite time on this planet and accentuate the sense of purpose of our life directions.

They say that there is no meaning in life save for the meaning that *you* give to it. Well, if that is true, then the 3 eulogies would germinate that meaning and even fortify your *ikigai*[63] for your life. Or, to paraphrase Sir Winston Churchill's words, *you would be impatient for the morning.* The profound quote attributed to Mark Twain—There are 2 most important days in our lives, the day we were born, and the day we find out *why*—resonates with the compelling need to articulate the 3 eulogies. Also, if you think about it, the cogent and clear reason for living would then fuel your motivation, which further spins the 3M that I espouse in Chapter 2.

If you think that this is not a necessary self-discovery, that it is an optional neat task that you would do when you are more settled down or when you are very free and have nothing to do, then consider this: Say I ask you to build me a chair. Go ahead and build it. You would immediately retort by saying, "Now, wait a minute, what *kind* of chair would you like me to build? Would it be a rocking chair, an office chair, a swivel chair, a wooden classic café chair, an all-weather garden chair, a wheelchair, an electric chair, a massage chair, a fine-dining chair, a stackable chair, a foldable wooden chair, etc?" And if I don't specify my requirements or specifications to you, you will have a problem building the chair that I want. Then again, suppose I tell you to go with the flow and see what comes out and build with what you have, so long as it is within my specific budget. Would that work? Well, up to a clumsy point and a rather mismatched product, most likely. If that drives home the message of the need for a clear blueprint as a prerequisite for a meaningful product, then ask yourself this: How much MORE is your LIFE worth compared to the chair?

---

[63] Japanese Okinawa's mantra- simply put, the reason you get up in the morning (The reason for living).

You know how in a movie or a TV series, when a certain character is confronted with a terminal illness (be it cancer or other types of incurable diseases), typically the attending doctor would then sombrely advise that patient to *"get his or her affairs in order"*. Well, essentially it means that you should get important documents (Will, titles, assets listing) in order or speak to your next-of-kin or loved one(s) on your impending demise. It is also a diplomatic way for the attending doctor to convey the *imminence* of death to the patient. It is a piece of sound advice, as not getting one's affairs in order would be unsettling and challenging for those attending to your earthly possessions and testamentary wishes after you are gone. Now, in the larger scheme of things, what if you also get your True North affairs (aka the 3 eulogies) in order while you still have a lot of life and bountiful energy within you? If you do that, your life will be more focused and enriching, and I will dare say more fun and driven.

A lot of people have expressed regrets towards the end of their lives on the things that they ought to have done, things that they should have said or not said, or relationships that should have been mended or reconciled or severed. The 3 eulogies will, in many ways, minimise these regrets because your life will be congruent with your true life's blueprint. Don't live in regrets, but live with the true and honest purposes (as encoded in the 3 eulogies) that resonate with your core values. Interestingly, Bronnie Ware, a palliative carer, wrote in her famous book *Top 5 Regrets of the Dying*[64], and the 1st in the list is this: *I wish I'd had the courage to live a life true to myself, not the life others expected of me.* The other list by Grace Bluerock[65] (social worker involved in hospice care) listed 9 items, and the first item states this: *"I wish I had been more loving to the people who matter the most."* William Shakespeare puts it well in Hamlet[66], *This above all else, to thine own self be true…*

"Death is not the greatest loss in life. The greatest loss is what dies inside us while we live."
– Norman Cousins

---

[64] *The Top Five Regrets of the Dying- A life Transformed by the Dearly Departed* (2012), By Bronnie Ware, an Australian author based in Sydney.
[65] Social worker in Murfreesboro, Tennessee, USA.
[66] Act 1 Scene 3

Incidentally, for those of you who are frightened by the thought of death or consider it taboo to talk about, the death café [67] phenomenon is a good place to join to encourage a safe and non-judgmental environment to talk about the subject of death. My focus here is on the event of death as the focal point, not necessarily the afterlife (if any, and which will be another explosive spiritual discourse), but the end point of life as living on this Earth is concerned. Death is inevitable and a certainty (apart from tax), as they say. So instead of avoidance, take the bull by the horns. Respect death as part of the reality of living and the death cycle. There is the beginning (called birth), and there is the endpoint (called death, demise, or passing away). Indeed, the sanctity of life is accentuated by the certainty, inevitability, and unavoidability of death. And here's another perspective to ponder: You may be able to work out your NTA [68] or how much money you have right now (to the last cent/penny), but in all honesty, you would not be able to tell how long you will be able to live.

"Do not fear death so much but rather the inadequate life."
– Bertolt Brecht

To further neutralise the morbidity of death as a subject matter, apparently, in Bhutanese culture, one is expected to think about death 5 times a day, and by no coincidence, Bhutan is consistently ranked as one of the happiest countries in the world. (They even started the concept of the Gross Happiness Index way back in 1973, in contradistinction to the GDP and Gross Development Index). It seems that death is a psychologically threatening fact, but when people contemplate it mindfully and respectfully, it brings a true perspective of the fragility and the gift of life, which conceivably helps the Bhutanese people to live more contented, fulfilled, and happier lives.

And if you have articulated your end in your mind, would it be a happy one, a successful one, or both?

---

[67] Started by Jon Underwood (UK), after he was inspired by the Swiss sociologist Bernard Crettaz, who organised the first Death Mortel in 2004. The Death Café phenomenon has spread to at least 66 countries.
[68] Net Tangible Asset.

CHAPTER 8

HAPPINESS & SUCCESS

The Earth was the centre of the universe. Period. That was the *gospel truth* up to the 15th century when science and especially astronomy were not so advanced yet. Of course, you wake up in the morning, you see the Sun rise from the east, and in the evening, you witness the Sun setting in the west while the Earth remains "stationary". The daily visual *evidence* is obvious. It didn't help that the Roman Catholic Church then was also preaching the theme of the Earth being the centre of the universe. Then came the Polish astronomer Nicholas Copernicus[69] (1473-1543), who propounded his heliocentric system, which put the Sun as the centre of our solar system. And it was Galileo Galilei [70], who in 1610 proved that the Sun is truly the centre, and the Earth (together with various other planets) revolves around the Sun. If that is the case, then we humans are no longer the centre or focal point of God's creation and are demoted to a more insignificant position inhabiting the 3rd rock from the Sun[71]. Galileo reaffirmed the Heliocentrism theory by Copernicus. The Roman Catholic Church was upset that mankind and the Earth were no longer the focal point, and via the Roman Inquisition in 1615, concluded that Heliocentrism was foolish, absurd, and heretical as it contradicted the Holy Scripture. In fact, Galileo was put under house arrest as a result of this discovery.

---

[69] On the Revolution of the Celestial Spheres- published in 1543

[70] Italian Astronomer (1564-1642)- The father of observational Astronomy.

[71] Well, technically, 4th rock- as Scientists just recently discovered the fastest orbiting asteroid orbiting the Sun. It is nearest to the Sun, overtaking Mercury's uno's position. It orbits the Sun in just 113 days.

Fun fact: The Earth spins around its axis at about 1,600 km/hour at the Equator. And for those of you who want to impress your science nerd friends, the Earth's rotation slows down about 2.3 milliseconds for every century.

You are probably wondering by now what the heck the Earth revolving around the Sun has to do with the topic of happiness. Maybe it is some cosmic force that I am about to introduce into the concept of happiness, or that the planetary alignment or the lunar rotation around the Earth would affect our moods. Nothing of that sort. The intriguing fact of the shift from the Sun revolving around the Earth to the correct version of the Earth revolving around the Sun took quite a while and a whole generation during Galileo's time and thereafter to reorientate their thinking and mindset about how the solar system works. Why? Because the people then were so used to the idea and the *given fact* that the Earth *had* to be the centre of the universe, no doubt fuelled by the indoctrination of the Roman Catholic Church then.

Now, back to the topic of happiness, it has been literally drummed into many of us since young, that if you want to be happy, first be successful; then only you will be happy. Make sense, isn't it? That is a *given fact*. Nothing to dispute. Look at all the miserable people around you. They are not successful, right? That again proved the *established* causality that *before* you get happiness, you must be successful first. And by the same *logic*, if you are not successful, you will then be miserable. This *established* cause and effect is also fortified by the *consistent* observation that typically, winners are happy, and losers are sad in any competitive sports. Victory is ecstasy, and defeat is gloomy. Case closed.

Not quite. Recent investigations into the science of happiness have revealed an erroneous understanding of our causality. First, some history. Previously, when psychology and psychiatry became mainstream branches of the scientific domain, the primary and predominant focus was on the mental illness of patients and the negative aspects of well-being, such as aberrant behaviours, depression, and the like. Then, in the last 20 to 30 years, the focus shifted to why some people cope better with crises and tragedies, and why some people tend to be more upbeat about life than others. Hence, the growth of positive psychology. So, instead of focusing on what's wrong with people, the attention was shifted to why certain types of people are happy, able to handle stress better, and what makes them successful in their lives despite the various challenges they encounter.

One of the epiphany moments for positive psychology is that it is not successful people who become happy, but rather that it is happy people who become successful. The sequencing or causality has been reversed. This is so disorientating for those who have been continuously programmed to think and believe that happiness is the rainbow earned when you are truly successful. Similar to the Earth-Sun centre of the universe debate in the 15th century, the success-happiness debate requires a tremendous mindset shift in today's society. The other complicating factor is also the way we define this rather subjective and overused word called *success*.

So for a proper contextual discourse on Happiness-Success, we need to properly define and tackle this glittering and yet controversial concept called *success*. Simply put, success is the achievement of something that we desire or aim for. Or is it? Somehow that is not the complete picture. For one, there are many so-called *successful* people who are literally lonely and miserable. This also challenges the whole success-will-get-you-happiness proposition. In this aspect, it was rather wise of the late Dr. Stephen Covey to avoid fuelling the controversy by not calling his seminal self-improvement book *The 7 Habits of Highly Successful People*. Anyway, just to massage the discussion further, have a look at the **Appendix** at the end of this eBook for some rather diverse definitions of success (in random order) for reflection and variety.

As you can see from the Appendix, there are so many versions and perspectives when it comes to defining success. Some are very grand, some are rather superficial, some are enriching, some are sacrificial and giving, some are minimalist, and some are personal. In the end, it is rather individualistic and situational. Should we try to compare the different versions and the various manifestations of success around us, it can either inspire us or the reference anxiety may seep in. Also, success can be multi-dimensional or even seasonal in some sense. If you merely put on your financial spectacles or binoculars and nothing else, then Warren Buffet and Bill Gates are SUPER successful, and Mahatma Gandhi and Mother Teresa failed miserably. You get the point. On this, the great Albert Einstein has an insightful perspective; he said, *"Do not try to be a person of success, but try to be a person of value."* Profound indeed. In a sense, success is what society judges or evaluates you by and is very much external, but value is much more fulfilling and enriching.

Anyway, among the various definitions of success, I find this generic definition to be the most inclusive, non-controversial, non-judgemental, and resonant with Kaizen: ***Success is the progressive realisation of a worthy goal(s)***. *Progressive* because life is a journey and not a destination, and *worthy* as something each individual should define nobly and authentically, which should be congruent with his or her 3 eulogies. So, planning a heist, robbing a bank, or creating an online and sophisticated dark network to distribute illicit drugs, however lucrative, would be repulsive to the virtuous definition of success.

Now that we are all on the same page with the *generic* definition of success (hopefully), let's get back to the causality and intertwine the concepts of happiness and success. In my opinion, the 2 main contributors to this revolutionary mindset change are Ben Tal-Shahar and Shawn Anchor. Ben Tal-Shahar studied and works at Harvard University, and he created arguably the most popular course in that university, you guessed it, relating to the subject of happiness (Positive Psychology). Shawn Anchor is from Texas, also from Harvard, and he considers Ben Tal-Shahar to be his mentor.

To Ben Tal-Shahar, happiness is the ultimate currency. He was Israel's national under-16 champion for squash, but he shared that he was only happy for a very short period of time. When he got into Harvard University, he thought it would be filled with happy students because they had made it to one of the most prestigious universities in the world. However, he observed that many of these *creme de la creme* students were not so happy either. In fact, statistically, the number of Harvard students experiencing depression was alarming. These observations intrigued him, and after his graduation, he approached his academic superior to start a course relating to happiness (Positive Psychology). The supervisor was encouraging but cautious about this rather *unconventional course*. The first attempt was a flop, and the turnout was miserable. Long story short, it became THE most popular course at Harvard at one point.

If you think about it, the association of happiness with success is natural. When we win a court case, secure a lucrative deal for our company, buy a new house, or our sweetheart says yes to our proposal for marriage, we celebrate… and sometimes even with gusto and all the confetti! We have grand dinners, champagnes, get-togethers, and lots of happy faces in WhatsApp photos, Facebook, and Instagram. And from an observational point of view, happiness is then associated with success. That is great. However, mere correlation does not explain the causality. The problem is the cause-and-effect dynamics. It also does not help that most advertisements that lure you into buying their products (be it a luxurious car, household gadget, or the next beauty product) will subtly convey the message that you are not happy or complete until you have purchased the product(s), and then reinforce the subliminal message by the *perfect* happiness after-effect[72].

And because of the erroneous presumption (that one needs to be successful to *earn or arrive at* the state of jubilation and happiness), we subconsciously *postpone* the state of happiness until we think we have *arrived* at the destination of success (which in itself is another short-lived version of chasing the rainbow for many *destinations*). Change the sequencing, and the qualitative approach of our daily lives becomes more enriching, and the best part it will optimise the progressive realisation of our worthy goal.

Of course, we all prefer happiness over sadness. Who doesn't? However, in the context of mindset, can we *choose* happiness over sadness? It's being said that happiness is a state of mind. I agree. Charles Swindoll said that life is 10% what happens to us and 90% how we respond to it. Terrific mindset. Of course, there will be tragedies, accidents, and setbacks that do make us sad. It is okay to be sad, and Ben Tal-Shahar affirms that it is part of our range of human emotions that we should acknowledge and embrace. I totally concur. Happiness cannot be mechanically *put on* to mask a sad situation. The key point, however, is not to let it unduly prolong and overwhelm us to the point of dejected defeat and destructive behaviour.

And once we recognise that happiness is a state of mind and that it *ought* to be the precursor to success, we should make a concerted attempt to boost our personal happiness index, so to speak. We should focus on things that make us happy, avoid gossip that generates envy and negative feelings, avoid comparison, and participate in activities that increase our dopamine and endorphin, like a morning walk, Shirin Yoko[73], gym routine, charity work,

---

72 See Chapter 10 on *Wabi Sabi* on this issue too.
73 Japanese term for forest bathing, which studies the beneficial effects of the phenomenon to our physical and mental health and well-being, from the tree-oil therapy of Phytoncides that strengthen our immune system to the mental calmness effect, among other things.

decluttering, and self-care. In another sense, happiness is not just a state of mind; it can be an active and conscious choice. And what your mind dwells on expands. We watch over our self-talk to ensure that we focus on the glass half-full and learn to see the humorous side of life. The ability to let go, to forgive, and not to expect perfection are also essential ingredients to nurture a happy demeanour[74]. We choose comedy shows more frequently. Speaking of comedy, the great comedian Charlie Chaplin was right when he said, *"A day without laughter is a day wasted."*

Fun Tip:
Bananas are a happy fruit as they have tryptophan, which gets converted into serotonin in the body, makes you more relaxed, improves your mood, and generally makes you feel happier. Just don't *go bananas* over it. ☺

Back to the revelation that happiness is the precursor to success. Simply put, a happy person will invariably be more successful. He or she will have a more pleasant and congenial personality to deal with, and he or she will attract good business opportunities or career advancement. He or she will have better health too. Better health leads to better productivity. Remember Norman Cousins who cured himself through the laugh/humour therapy and is attributed with the adage Laughter is the best medicine? This is what he said: "Laughter serves as a blocking agent. Like a bulletproof vest, it may help protect you against the ravages of negative emotions that can assault you in disease." Well said, Norman Cousins! It is also trite that toxic stress not only robs us of our health with the secretion of cortisol hormone but also impairs our optimal productivity, creativity, and general sense of well-being. Cultivation of a happy attitude and cheerful demeanour is a good tonic against toxic stress.

---

74 See Chapter 10 on *Wabi Sabi*, which deal with the pernicious effect of perfectionism.

Just to be sure we don't get the wrong message, being happy *per se* does not automatically make you successful. There are other essential contributing factors, like creating value for people, grit, productive work, and meaningful collaborative effort, that lead to success. All these, properly nurtured and combined, will create a wonderful momentum to fuel you towards your worthy goal, be it to be financially free, have better health, cultivate a strong working team, or help out in some charities. But fundamentally, the precursor and the fuel that sustains that momentum[75] would be the habitual conditioning of the mind to be in a happy state. To state the obvious, try to be miserable most of the time, and then focus on your deep work or task at hand. Very challenging, I would bet. Interestingly, a slouched posture can even get us into an unhappy state, according to Anthony Robbins as he observes that people who are down and miserable tend to slouch and look down. So he advocates that *physiology* affects psychology too. Wonderful stuff. Use it and apply it. Stand straight, be confident, and be happy.

"Success is not the key to happiness. Happiness is the key to success."
– Albert Schweitzer

The nagging question that follows then is, how exactly do we cultivate and sustain the conditioning and state of happiness? Some would argue that it is in our innate personality that some people by nature are upbeat about life, some are more melancholic, and then there are some who are *serious* most of the time. Well, Sonja Lyubomirsky (Russian migrant to the USA), a professor from the University of California, has written a wonderful book called *The How of Happiness*[76] wherein she listed the 7 things that can improve your state of happiness anytime in your life:

1. Do something nice for someone else (altruism)
2. Give THANKS on a regular basis (gratitude)[77]
3. Cultivate an optimistic outlook on life (glass-half-full mindset)
4. Avoid invidious social comparisons (don't compare)
5. Nurture your relationships (stay connected)

---

[75] See Chapter 2 on this exciting topic called "Momentum".
[76] Published 2007, By Prof Sonja Lymbomirsky, BA (Harvard University) PhD in Social Psychology (Stanford University). Her subsequent book is called *The Myth of Happiness*.
[77] More of this in the next Chapter.

6. Enjoy your work (passion in vocation)
7. Take care of your body (self-care)

Professor Sonja also advocates that the environment (10%) and set-points (50%) only contribute 60% to our happiness, and up to 40% is entirely in our hands—the conceptual approach of *Intentional Activity,* as she calls it. Same mindset with Charles Swindoll, except Charles's 90% is even more upbeat about the Circle of Control[78] of his life. Professor Sonja defines happiness as "the experience of joy, contentment, or positive well-being, combined with a sense that one's life is good, meaningful, and worthwhile."

Speaking of contentment, there is a famous Chinese idiom, 知足常乐, or 知足常樂. Meaning, that if one understands contentment, one will always be happy. In Japanese culture, the equivalent quote would be *"ware tada taru o shiru,"* which literally means *"I only know plenty"*, and contextually means that *"rich is the person who is content with what they have"* or *"I have everything I need."* The Greek philosopher Epictetus hit the nail on its head with this profound quote: *"Wealth consists not in having great possessions, but in having few wants."* On that note, I would like to add one more thing to the 7 items above:

8. Be contented

In 1921, Albert Einstein won the Nobel Physics Prize for the Theory of Relativity. The following year, he visited Japan for a lecture series. The story is told that a bellboy came to make a delivery to his hotel room. However, instead of giving the bellboy a monetary tip, Albert Einstein gave him a handwritten note, personally signed by himself. The debate is still out as to whether Albert was out of loose change at that time, or he wanted to pass something *of value* to the bellboy. Well, the debate aside, that handwritten note was sold for US $1.56 million by one of the bellboy's descendants in 2017. What did the note say? Here it is:

"A calm and modest life brings more happiness than the pursuit of success combined with constant restlessness."

---

[78] See Chapter 11 on this amazing mind-set.

In Neil Pasricha's[79] 2016 book entitled *The Happiness Equation*[80], the author listed 7 things to be happy, some of which overlap with Professor Sonja's list, viz. *gratitude*, random acts of kindness, and being physically active. Neil also talks about being in the Flow, unplugging from social media, and meditation. The takeaway message from Neil is really encouraging in that *you can learn to be happier.* And it is not so much an either/or, binary happy/sad compartmentalisation, but more of consciously moving from sadness to happiness on an emotional scale. And speaking of gratitude, the next chapter will connect you with happiness, the precursor of success. So in terms of sequencing, it would be Gratitude → Happiness → Success. Check it out in the next chapter.

Here's an actionable and doable happy tip: I love music. And music therapy to uplift our mood is amazing and measurable. So what I do is compile all my favourite music, be it jazz, classical, and happy upbeat evergreen songs on my MP3 player or my music app on my hand-phone. Then, when I go for my morning walks, hikes, or cycling[81], I let the music accompany my mind, and immediately, the mood is comparatively more upbeat and cheerful. Even when I work, it is either soft jazz or soothing classical music in the background. Try it. Create your playlist via *Spotify*, YouTube Music, or your own MP3 device and fill it with happy and upbeat songs. It will enhance your work routine and concentration, and give you more sustained deep focus and longer engagement, be it your exercise or your desk work.

Research has confirmed again that people who listen to music while working experience better efficiency, heightened creativity, a better mood, and improved focus. In fact, soothing music helps to relax the nervous and cardiovascular systems too. Incidentally, there is a subscription service called *Focus@Will* that claims to be neuroscience-based. It allows you to choose your music preferences, and its aim is to help you focus on your task at hand. One of their conceptual approaches is to use instrumental music, as lyrics can be distracting.

A very important reason why all public halls, theatres, factories, and conference rooms have their exit doors open outward is because of the painful

---

[79] Founder of Institute For Global Happiness
[80] "The How of Happiness" was also referred to in this book.
[81] Recommend using bone conduction earphones for safety reason.

lesson learned during a fire accident or instances of panic where the crowd or congregation presses against the doors, literally preventing the doors from being opened if the doors are designed to be opened only from the inside[82]. Hence, it is now a standard fire by-law requirement that all such exit doors must never be locked and open outward for safety reasons, given the herd behaviour observed during a panic or crisis situation. In short, they should open in the direction of the evacuation. And here is another mindset thought for happiness, that *the door to happiness opens outwards*[83]. Indeed, the Chinese have this expression, 助人为快乐之本, which literally means to help other people is the foundation of happiness. Now, go seek your happiness.

---

[82] 1883, Victoria Hall disaster in Sunderland, England more than 180 children died. 1911, 146 factory workers died in Triangle Shirtwaist Factory fire in New York city, USA.
[83] Attributable to Danish Philosopher, Soren Kiekegaard (1813-1855)

CHAPTER 9

GRATITUDE

Thank you! Terima kasih! 謝謝! Merci! Vielen Dank! धन्यवाद!
ありがとうございました

Gracias! ขอบคุณ! Tack! 감사합니다! Grazie! Gratia! Tak! Salamat!
Спасибо! Cảm ơn bạn!

NB: The word gratitude is derived from the Latin word Gratia, which means grace, graciousness, or gratefulness (depending on the context).

Thank You can be said in so many different languages in the world. It's a beautiful phrase that has such an alluring reflection of us as fellow human beings. Its universal meaning is *not* ambiguous; it is used to express appreciation and gratitude for a gift, some altruistic act, kindness or some wonderful situation prevailing to the person. And that expression is a manifestation of gratitude. If we do it, people say that we are being grateful, and conversely, if we don't do it, especially after receiving the gift or kind act, people say that we are being ungrateful. By the way, THANK YOU for buying and reading this book. Now, what has this sense of gratitude got to do with mental toughness?

4 interconnected reasons. The first has to do with happiness; secondly, gratitude impacts the body-mind connection that we talked about in Chapter 4. The third reason is the social dynamic of gratitude. And the

fourth reason is that life is a gift. We will address the 4 interconnected reasons as follows.

First, the interconnect with happiness. A daily gratitude practice has been demonstrated to significantly improve our happiness. Think about it: The Thanksgiving season somehow uplifts our spirits. Why and how does it work? In fact, Positive Psychology research has observed that gratitude is consistently associated with an increase in happiness.

Scanning through the timelines, one can be grateful for the past (recalling positive events, achievements, meaningful encounters, near-death experiences, etc.), the present (contentment, health, financial and food security, good family and friends), and the future (plans for travel, moving to a new home, hope for wonderful adventures).

Various top universities have done some studies which demonstrated the association between gratitude and happiness, although the cause and effect are still open for discussion[84]. Nonetheless, the association is irrefutable, in that people who consciously count their blessings tend to be happier and less depressed.

Secondly, the body-mind connection. Practising gratitude will improve sleep, boost immunity and consequently decrease the risk of diseases. Research has even confirmed that gratitude improves our mental health. Just imagine, in our pill-popping culture, there is a pill that can increase your happiness, improve your sleep, boost your immune system, and enhance your physical health. Well, there is none. The good news is that *gratitude* is the health tonic that will do all that, with no adverse effects, but with all the goodness that I have just mentioned. The best part? It is free. The trick is to be able to consciously tap into it regularly. In fact, for those of us who have problems sleeping (for the technically inclined, it is called insomnia), count your blessings after you snuggle into your warm bed or make a point to journal your daily gratitude before you hit the bed, and see how your sleep routine (aka circadian rhythm) improves.

Thirdly, it will enhance our social interactions. The bottom line is people like people who are grateful and shun people who are ungrateful. From a

---

[84] Attributable to Danish Philosopher, Soren Kiekegaard (1813-1855)

sociological perspective, grateful people are much more congenial to get along with, as they tend to be less offensive, more appreciative even of tiny gestures, well-mannered, and generally do not take things for granted. Ungrateful people see the glass as half empty, typically are not appreciative of kind gestures, and tend to be rather self-centred. No wonder Cicero [85] said that *"Gratitude is the greatest of virtues, and the parent of all other virtues."*

Fourthly, our attitude to life.

If you think about it, this life of yours is truly a wonderful gift. The famous Oxford University Professor of Biology, Professor Richard Dawkins puts it ever so eloquently in his book *"Unweaving the Rainbow: Science, Delusion and Appetite for Wonder"*[86]:

"We are going to die, and that makes us the lucky ones. Most people are never going to die because they are never going to be born. The potential people who could have been here in my place but who will, in fact, never see the light of day outnumber the sand grains of Arabia. Certainly, those unborn ghosts include greater poets than Keats, and scientists greater than Newton. We know this because the set of possible people allowed by our DNA so massively exceeds the set of actual people. In the teeth of these stupefying odds, it is you and I, in our ordinariness, that are here. We privileged few, who won the lottery of birth against all odds, how dare we whine at our inevitable return to that prior state from which the vast majority have never stirred?"

And the appropriate way we treat a gift is with *immense* gratitude. And in this wonderful phenomenon called life—with all its mysteries, energy, and discoveries for us to enjoy and enrich our lives—it is only proper for us to have profound respect and reverence for the gift of life. This mindful, humble, and respectful approach to daily living should also extend to fellow human beings for their gift of life too. This mindset is further reinforced in our daily living, where our 3 eulogies are clearer by the day.

---

[85] Marcus Tullius Cicero- 106 BC – 43 BC, orator and statesman of Ancient Rome.
[86] Published in 1998, in which the author discusses the relationship between science and the arts from the perspective of a scientist.

We can also cultivate the habit of practising gratitude through daily or frequent gratitude journaling. You can either do it through the premium Moleskine notebook, a simple comb-bound journal book or like me, through any digital phone app that supports easy entry of notes. As and when you are free or feel that negativity is seeping into your brain, read through your gratitude list. It will uplift your mood and remind you of how wonderful your treasured life has been.

Gratitude Breathing. Breath in itself is a profound manifestation that we *are* alive. And a lot has been written about the power and health benefits of deep breathing. In fact, the Chinese ancient art of *Chi Kung* [气公], literally means the art of breath. And there are even testimonies of how Chi Kung, properly practised, had helped to cure cancer. Indeed, the COVID-19 pandemic has in, so many ways, accentuated the fact that so many of us have taken our breath for granted. Those patients who had been severely infected by the COVID-19 virus to the point where they needed the medical assistance of a ventilator and/ or oxygen would certainly give me a resounding YES! Now, if we combine the power of deep breathing with the transformational power of expressing gratitude, the synergy is phenomenal.

**"The best thinking has been done in solitude.
The worst has been done in turmoil."**
– Thomas Edison

In my regular solitude and reflection during my morning routine, I have been able to combine the transformational power of gratitude with my practice of deep breathing. And I would like to share the simple process of gratitude breathing for your benefit and well-being.

[Yours Truly on the big rock* at a nearby reserved forest, after my Shirin Yoko.]

*That rock is affectionately called the Dinosaur Egg as it resembles a gigantic egg. And I sometimes crack a hard-boiled chicken egg on that Dinosaur Egg to mindfully enjoy that simple egg with all its life-giving nutrients[87] and to be thankful for life right after I have finished my gratitude breathing.

The idea is to sit as comfortably and quietly as possible in an isolated or minimally distracting spot and gradually settle down your mind and body.

---

[87] Apparently, an Egg is a complete food, with all the essential nutrients, save for Vitamin C.

Then, in a gentle way, be present and acknowledge your breath. With your 10 fingers as a guide, place your right palm of your hand on your right knee and your left palm of your left hand on your left knee. [One tap for one thing grateful until you reach 10 things you are grateful for. If time permits, repeat the 10 taps cycle with persons, new moments, or events to be grateful for.] Once you are consciously aware of your breath, gradually and consciously take a deep and slow breath—slowly breathe in and breathe out. During that in-out rhythm, focus on *one* grateful thought. Relish that thought and happily be grateful for it. If you have any troubled thought(s) or unresolved conflict at that moment, don't fight it or try to resolve it. Acknowledge it and get back to your Circle of Control[88] and be present. The unresolved thought will pass. Focus your mind on things or events you want to be grateful for. Alternatively, you can mentally create a capsule or a KIV file for the unresolved thought or situation and let your mind know that you will deal with them after your gratitude breathing session.

That single thought can be anything that happened recently—a wonderful event, a small victory, a beautiful message from a friend, your parent's health, your child's health, your health, the gift of breath, the beautiful weather, the fact that you are alive, the legs that carried you to that serene spot, the nutritious meal that you just had, the ability to see with your eyes, the funny movie that you watched last night, the roof over your head, the fact that you could find a parking spot, the stranger who opened the door for you, good friends, a kind deed done to you, a kind deed done to a stranger, a near-death experience that reminded you of the fragility of life, your spouse or life partner who loves you, the neighbour who gave you a basket of apples, etc. The thought could be big or small. No specific order. It could be profound, or it could be a tiny moment of bliss or even a comical encounter. The idea is to develop a gratitude mindset to sync with your deep breathing.

Once the in-out rhythm is done for one breath, use the tip of your first finger on your right hand (or left hand, if you are left-handed) to very gently touch your knee to indicate that one thought is bundled in gratitude. Repeat the in-out rhythm for the remaining 9 fingers/thumbs, for 9 beautiful and cherished thoughts/events that you want to express your gratitude. If time is a factor, 10 breaths for the 10 fingers/thumbs would constitute one cycle of gratitude breathing (a habit-forming routine). And if you have more time, then repeat the

---

88 See Chapter 11 on this fascinating concept.

cycle, using your fingers' touch as a guide that syncs with the in-out breath, until you are in a state of wonderful tranquillity and a calm state of mind.

And for those of you who want to fine-tune the deep breathing to a more effective mode, try abdominal breathing (i.e., breathing with the aid of the diaphragm, and allowing the stomach area/abdomen to expand naturally, rather than the chest), as it is more natural for our physiology. Not convinced? Observe a baby or a toddler when he or she sleeps and see if the chest expands, or the abdomen expands.

The key point to note is to take it as gently and as slowly as possible and develop a habitual routine. This is not a finite course. It is an unhurried journey. Consistent with the limitless mindset, you are not in any competition or test. It is your unhurried and happy journey to develop the Kaizen of gratitude breathing. It does wonders for your body-mind connection, and I will bet that you will be a happier and calmer person, and your ability to focus and solve the day's challenges will be truly empowered. It's been said that being calm is a superpower. I venture to say that it is because we think clearer and are more focused when we are calm. You may not be indestructible, but you will be more *indistractable.*

"When you feel like life is out of focus, always return to the basics of life. Breathing. No breath, no life."
– Mr. Miyagi (the Japanese martial art teacher in Karate Kid)

CHAPTER 10

WABI SABI-EMBRACING IMPERFECTIONS AND IMPERMANENCES IN LIFE

Perfect 10[89]! The world was stunned. Nadia Elena Comaneci, the Romanian gymnast, was the first Olympian ever to be awarded a perfect score of 10.0 for gymnastics at the 1976 Olympic Games. Speaking of perfection, the world-famous statue of David in Italy by Michelangelo is also considered a perfect statue as it depicts physical perfection. Giorgio Vasari (16th-century artist and historian) exclaimed that "no other artwork is equal to it in any respect!" The story goes that when the statue of David was finally completed, Michelangelo cried because there was nothing else he could do to improve upon it.

Is the pursuit of perfectionism good for us? Well, you can argue that if Nadia and Michelangelo could do it, so should we, and so can we. Full disclosure: I am not perfect. To be fair, many inorganic things and structures can be perfect, such as a perfect sphere, a perfect ball bearing, a perfect waterproofed water bottle or a perfectly symmetrical drawing. In fact, the demands of certain complex machines require high-end precision engineering tools to make perfect ball bearings to ensure that the rotational movements are super-smooth. However, many organic things are not that perfect or symmetrical, such as the shapes of fruits and leaves, birth defects, and the ageing or oxidative process of living things.

---

[89] The fact that this Chapter is also Chapter 10 is purely coincidental.

The debate is this: Is the pursuit of perfection noble or to be encouraged by us? Those of us who are perfectionists in personality, upbringing, and mindset would totally support that argument. Incidentally, the upmarket brand of Toyota, Lexus, has a posh tagline that says, *The relentless pursuit of perfection*. In essence, it accentuates the pursuit of the micro-details of the car design and the engineering dynamics to the point of perfection. It was Toyota's corporate strategy to take on the German luxurious automobile players. At the time of writing, Toyota was the richest automobile company in the world, and it overtook Mercedes-Benz to become the world's most valuable automobile company in 2021. In the corporate world, it has done exceedingly well. Nice. At the same time, in Japan, there is a concept called *Karoshi*, which means death from over-working, literally speaking. Do you know how your dad or mum used to tell you that hard work will not kill you? Well, the Japanese have successfully debunked this parental advice. The working culture (aka workaholism) in Japan can be punishing, and for that matter, the rest of Asia too. Another common physiological manifestation is a heart attack or stroke. And the consistent medical advice for the last 30 years is that stress is a silent killer.

Indeed, in the context of optimal mental health, it is my experience, observation and conviction that it is more harmful in the long run to have a perfectionist mindset. The reframing of the mindset should be to pursue excellence, not perfection[90]. This is because excellence resonates with Kaizen's concept of *continuous* improvement, whereas perfection signifies that you have completed the task or achieved the peak or its limit, and there is nothing else to be improved upon. The problem is that perfectionism is a stressful mindset. And to the perfectionist, it is still not perfect; hence, he or she cannot stop and be happy with the progress. Whereas an excellentist[91] is able to pause and enjoy the progress and relish in the Kaizen of improvement, yet mindfully acknowledging the fact that he or she is not striving for perfection, but excellence. Indeed, we are all work-in-progress, and the journey of life is not a perfect ride.

In Chemistry, there is a principle of nature called the law of entropy, which essentially means that things will invariably get into disorder. Why so?

---

[90] If the top management of Lexus is reading this, you may wish to adapt your tagline to "the relentless pursuit of excellence".

[91] Hopefully Oxford Dictionary will admit this beautiful word one day.

From a pure chemical lens, entropy is a measure of the tendency to disorder—quantifying how dispersed the energy is among the particles in a system. Organically, ageing can be an irreversible process of entropy accumulation, and death would be the ultimate disorder, a state of maximum entropy. Acceptance of this law of entropy is truly embracing the concept of *Wabi-sabi*. Let's investigate this wonderful Japanese philosophy.

In true perspective, life is imperfect in its various multitude of manifestations. If that is so trite, then why do we hear common phrases like perfect health, perfect body, perfect beauty, perfect holiday, perfect couple, perfect car, perfect marriage and the like being thrown around without any objections? This has to do with our worship and adoration of perfectionism, no doubt fuelled by the barrage of advertising bombardment, which subliminally conveys the message that the perfect [fill in the blank] is attainable. If you learn to observe and analyse many of these advertisement messages, perfection is the ideal or desired outcome and leads to happiness and epitomises success[92]. Apart from the constant stress of striving for perfectionism, we feel short-changed or discontented with our self-image and present conditions in life simply because they are not perfect yet. This has a pernicious effect on our self-worth, self-acceptance and true enjoyment of our daily living, especially when we consciously or subconsciously postpone our happiness until we supposedly arrive at our perfect destination or accomplishment.

This is where I learned the beautiful philosophy of *Wabi-sabi*, a Japanese concept that is not easy to explain in a non-Japanese context. Nevertheless, in essence, it is the art of embracing impermanence and accepting imperfection as part of life's true beauty. In essence, *Wabi-sabi* teaches us to acknowledge and embrace the impermanence and imperfection in our lives, and to learn to appreciate the beauty of nature in its glorious imperfection and the fragility of our daily lives. Acceptance and forgiveness become second nature rather than disappointment and frustration.

The often-told story that epitomises the concept of *Wabi-sabi* is how the Japanese people would actually use molten gold to mend a broken bowl and still appreciate the mended bowl with the visible crack lines laced with gold[93]. If you think about it, using gold (a precious metal) to repair and mend a broken

---

92 This also result in postponed happiness. See Chapter 8 on this discussion.
93 *Kintsugi:* The Japanese art of repairing your pottery with gold.

bowl (that could have been thrown away) is a pretty mind-boggling concept. Artistically, *Kintsugi* truly teaches acceptance of imperfection. To be able to truly appreciate the beauty of a cracked bowl (being mended by gold) is true tranquillity in the stressful world of perfectionism. In nature, I observe with reverence the

free-flow, organic growth of trees, their branches, and even their asymmetrical leaves and veins that have their alluring beauty. Nothing predictable, and the variety continues to mesmerise our visual senses.

This last topic is crucial to optimise your mental fitness, as it provides the empowerment and safe ethos for you to fumble and embrace fallibility as you learn to *internalise* the other 9 concepts and systems. Now, imagine a perfectionist mindset trying to tackle and achieve the 9 concepts in the previous chapters. His or her self-worth will be crushed by negative self-talk, inconsistent habit-forming patterns, incorrect mindsets, destructive instant gratification, and the like. Giving up would be the next logical step as the *perfect score* is unattainable. This is where *Wabi-sabi* is so powerful and yet soothing in nurturing the grit and perseverance to continue the journey and to even relish the joy of the journey principally because of acceptance[94] of the imperfection and to embrace the process of incremental improvement (aka Kaizen) as the key focus.

Perfectionism can also *incubate* postponed or deferred action by waiting for the *perfect moment*. And if there is no attempt, then technically the perfect moment or result has not been ruined yet. The perceived perfect scenario is *protected*. The problem is decision paralysis occurs, and we think we are secured to our *safe zone* and waiting for the *perfect* moment to launch our project or mission. In the end, we postpone living. Reflecting upon my own

---

94 There is a beautiful Japanese word for acceptance: Uketamo- "I humbly accept with an open heart."

life, one of the reasons why my wife and I decided to have a child only after 10 years of our marriage was because I wasn't sure I would be a *good parent* (aka perfect parent). Imagine that! Good thing my wife and I had [95], and I thoroughly enjoyed our daughter's growing up years and the enrichment it brought to our family dynamics. Even for this eBook, I have been telling myself that I want to write a book, and the decision has been kicked down the road of life so many times. No time, no inspiration, fear of failure, you name it, and I would have imagined it. I was waiting for the *perfect moment* to start writing my eBook. For many years, I waited. Thanks to the embrace of *Wabi-sabi*, I have since jettisoned the illusive perfection mindset from my daily thoughts.

One of my recent favourite books on minimalism that helped me to take the plunge into writing this eBook is the book by the wonderful Japanese author named Fumio Sasaki entitled *Goodbye Things*[96]. This amazing cut-through-the-chase, no-frill Japanese author is truly an authentic and humble writer. He writes lucidly and transparently about his life, which is so alluring. And the English version, in plain vanilla English, is such a delight to read. One of his endearing messages is that because he is no longer defined by his possessions, he is truly free to do the things that matter most to him, including writing his rather straight-talk book entitled *Goodbye Things*. He shared about his pride in showing off possessions such as his book collection, camera collection, etc. (don't we all?), and how decluttering (saying goodbye to things) had helped him to be truly free, and he is no longer stressed by the constant need for comparison. The approach to decluttering was so elegantly simple and yet profound that it gave me another *aha* moment. In my view, Fumio's approach to minimalism and decluttering has taken Mario Kondo's decluttering to a whole new level. Anyway, to be fair, both have differing styles and approaches to minimalism and decluttering. Respect.

"The best way to find out what we really need is to get
rid of what we don't."
– Marie Kondo

---

95 Daughter named Julia Liow Hui Ting.
96 Published 2015. Fumio has written another follow-up book entitled "Hello, Habits: A minimalist Guide to a Better Life". 2019.

The other reason why decluttering is mentioned in this chapter is that, in many ways, perfectionism results in the accumulation of stuff. Why? The subliminal message from the advertising media is that until and unless you have *that* product, you are not complete or not perfect *yet*. So you work hard and buy that product. Then the *next* product is shouting for your attention and your credit card or eWallet. Desire and materialism take over your mind. Next thing we know, we are defined by our possessions (or the lack of it). *Wabi-Sabi* helps to detoxify the hoarding and the accumulation of stuff. As they say, less is more, and our home is a *living* space, not a storage space. And you are enough. Indeed, to be happy you don't need to be perfect. You just need to be authentically real and accept yourself as you are because you are already enough.

"Your worth consists in what you are and not in what you have."
– Thomas Edison

I have learned over the years to accept my imperfections, fallibility, and shortcomings. I hope that with *Wabi-sabi*, you can too. With acceptance comes the new energy to want to move forward with the daily Kaizen.

There is an old movie [97] about a grumpy meteorologist guy (acted by Bill Murray) who went to a small town called Punxsutawney to do a TV report and the next thing you know, he was living the exact same day over and over again, exactly from 6.00 am every morning. Every incident, every character, and every conversation could be predicted after a while. He could not break the repetition. Initially, he was baffled and confused. Then he became frustrated, reckless, cheeky, and even suicidal. Towards the last part of the movie, he was awakened to the epiphany that he could actually capitalise on the predictable daily repetition and improve his life (no doubt using Kaizen), his interpersonal relationships, and his contributions to the little community that had endeared to him. He took up piano lessons, ice carving, etc., and became quite accomplished in them. Long story short, he managed to make Andie MacDowell fall in love with him.

In fact, the takeaway message and the overall theme of the movie Groundhog Day are so profound that Paul Hannam (ex-adjunct Professor at

---

[97] **Groundhog Day** (1993) Starting Andie MacDowell as Rita, and Bill Murray as Phil Conners.

Oxford University) even wrote a book[98] to share how to improve your life, one day at a time. Simple pleasures in everyday life, shifting from autopilot to living life intentionally, the material me versus the authentic me—these are some of the good things distilled by Paul Hannam from the highest-grossing[99] movie of 1993. And in the context of Kaizen, if we mindfully have the mindset to improve by 1% every day, no matter how mundane or repetitive our days can be or how imperfect or impermanent our daily lives can be (the *Wabi-sabi* spirit), the meaningfulness and the ikigai will eventually be nurtured.

---

[98] **The Wisdom of Groundhog Day**, 2016.
[99] The movie earned over US$105 million.

CHAPTER 11

SUMMING-UP
THE INTERCONNECT AMONG THE STRATEGIES, AND THE INTEGRATED TIME-MANAGEMENT SKILLS TO APPLY THEM

I learned in my secondary school's biology that in our body, a group of cells functioning together is called a tissue, and a group of tissues functioning together is called an organ, and a group of organs functioning together is then called a system. And these systems, be it the digestive system, the respiratory system, the lymphatic system or the nervous system work in an integrated manner to sustain our daily lives. Our bodies are living miracles of the harmonious workings of all the intricate and complex systems. The previous chapter on the body-mind connection expanded quite a fair bit on the often-unnoticed communication between the 2. So it is with all the systems and strategies that I have advocated in the last 10 Chapters.

The integration of the 10 wonderful concepts and systems that I have explained earlier will bring about a *mental synergy* that will truly inoculate your mind against the various challenges and road bumps ahead of your life journey. It will not eliminate all your problems, but it will surely help you to tackle them and make better decisions when you adjust your mindset, use the Kaizen technique, and develop good habits, for example.

You see, the respiratory system cannot work in silos (don't want to distribute oxygen to other systems' cells), and the digestive system cannot say I won't share the nutrients that I have processed with the other organs. Similarly, learning Kaizen without appreciating the power of habits is missing the empowering synergy of using habits to generate momentum for Kaizen, and vice versa, that is using Kaizen to strengthen our good habits. And if you are not clear on your 3 eulogies, your habit-forming muscles will not be properly motivated. Grateful people are happy people, and happy people will optimise their opportunities for success. But if we don't see the big picture and go around with binocular vision, then our self-talk becomes myopic and destructive, and the next thing we know, the delayed gratification will invariably be replaced by instant gratification, which also messes up the body-mind equilibrium.

To further optimise our mindset to seize the day, I will share the integration of 3 profound concepts of self-management in the context of time management that will turbo-charge the way you apply the 10 strategies from the last 10 chapters. These 3 concepts are well-established time-management tools that are taught in many courses and management training programmes or seminars. The challenge here is to see the interrelation between the 3 concepts and properly integrate them into our daily lives. That's where the magic happens.

What are the 3 well-known concepts? Here they are (in no particular order):

1. The Circle of Control;
2. The 4 quadrants of time management; and
3. The 80/20 principle.

The 3 Circles of Our Decision-making Realm

The 3 Circles, as depicted below, illustrate the area of the decision-making realm that we can focus on, dabble in, or even soak ourselves in day in, day out. The outermost circle, called the Circle of Concern, would be things that we can be legitimately concerned with but we can't really control directly. The second inner circle is the Circle of Influence, where various issues and matters can be influenced by us, which is relatively better than the Circle of Concern, but we still do not have direct control. The innermost circle is called the Circle of Control. This is where we have the most direct control—on matters involving our response to a situation, event, problem, or even an opportunity.

"We must make the best of those things that are in our power, and take the rest as nature gives it."
– Epictetus

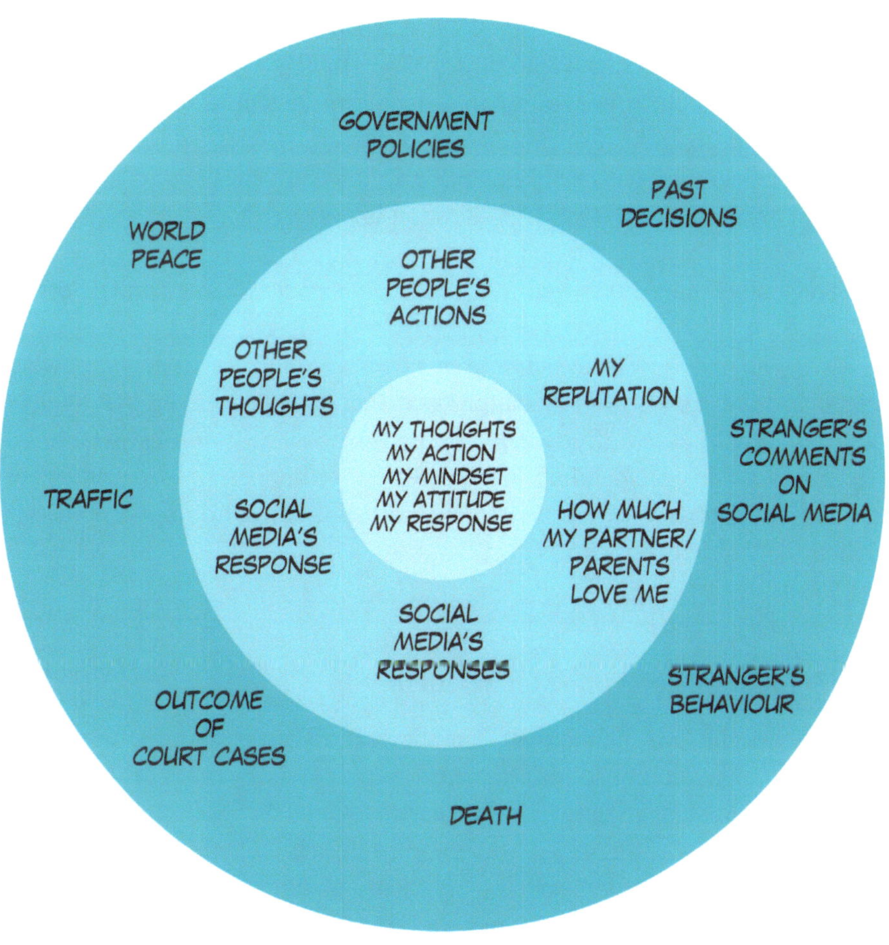

[the 3 Circles]

Our minds can move around freely around the 3 Circles and deal with them in no particular order, depending on what we focus on and our habitual thought process. The discipline here is to spend the *predominant* part of your day on the innermost Circle of Control. Why? This is because it is where you will have the most direct and *productive* control of your thought process and the manner in which you respond to any situation or event. The more you are able to focus your time and energy on the Circle of Control, the more centred and stress-free you will be. The explanation is rather simple: The more time you spend dealing with the Circle of Concern or even the Circle of Influence, the more you will realise that it will invariably generate anxiety and stress-related symptoms. Why? Because you have relatively less control over them compared to the innermost Circle of Control. The working definition of *stress* entails things that are beyond your control and over which you wish you had control (the vicious cycle then generates the *stressor* cortisol, and the stressful situation is *nurtured*).

The magic happens when you make a conscious and Kaizen effort to keep your thought process and energy in the Circle of Control. This is because you will realise the clarity of effective control, which empowers your calmness. Once you are calmer and more collected, you are able to move to the Circle of Influence to handle issues there, too. And whenever you feel that you are spending too much time or beginning to stress out in the Circle of Concern or Circle of Influence, you mindfully move yourself back to the Circle of Control.

The 4 Quadrants of Time Management

In the 1950s, the USA's President Eisenhower [100] had to manage a growing country that was fast becoming the next superpower in the world. One of the time-management strategies that he developed in managing his daily decision process was the 4-quadrants approach, which helped him to titrate and compartmentalise the myriad of issues (international or domestic) confronting him as the CEO of America. The following diagram depicts the 4 quadrants:

---

[100] Dwight Eisenhower (1890-1969), 34th US president (1953-1961)

	URGENT	NOT URGENT
IMPORTANT	**DO** DO IT NOW	**DECIDE** SCHEDULE A TIME TO DO IT
NOT IMPORTANT	**DELEGATE** WHO CAN DO IT FOR YOU?	**DELETE** ELIMINATE IT

The 4 Quadrants approach presumably assisted him in prioritising the hundreds of decision-making processes confronting him day in and day out. Dr. Stephen Covey also embraced it in his bestseller *The 7 Habits of Highly Effective People*, wherein he fine-tuned it further to tackle the tension between the urgent and the important. The takeaway message from Dr. Covey's approach is that the *important* should not be at the mercy of the *urgent*, and oftentimes, it is the urgent that sabotages the important. He, therefore, advocated that priority should be allocated to Quadrant II, which is where we should spend our predominant time. The diagram below illustrates this further.

Over the years, I have learned that *urgent* is invariably stressful, and it gives unfounded glory to *being busy* and egoistic self-importance, whereas *important* may not always have the *urgent* flavour to go with it at times and can even be less glamorous than *urgent*. Having understood the sheer importance of Quadrant II, I have since replaced *urgent* with clear timelines, using a realistic buffer to manage time-sensitive projects and assignments. This gives clarity to team members and redistributes the stress factor to the front-end rather than the popular *last-minute* rush and panic-driven drama. With the wildfire of *urgent* tamed, the mind then has more time and mental clarity to focus and prioritise the important matters in Quadrant II.

	URGENT	NOT URGENT
IMPORTANT	**1. DEMAND** • CRISIS • PRESSING PROBLEMS • DEADLINE PROJECTS	**2. THE ZONE** • PLANNING • GRATITUDE • RELATIONSHIP BUILDING • NEW OPPORTUNITIES • LEARNING, DEVELOPING NEW SKILLS
NOT IMPORTANT	**3. ILLUSION** • INTERRUPTIONS • SOME CALLS, MAILS • SOME MEETINGS • PRESSING MATTERS WITHOUT IMPACT • ATTENTION GRABBING ACTIVITIES	**4. ESCAPE** • TRIVIA, SOCIAL MEDIA SCROLLING • TIME WASTERS • SOCIAL CHIT-CHAT • INTERNET SURFING • PLEASANT ACTIVITIES

The other observation to make is that Quadrant I is where crisis management takes place. An emergency, an overlooked timeline, an accident, or even a catastrophe are obvious examples of Quadrant I scenarios. It is imperative that you deal with it with all your urgent attention and pumping adrenaline. Life happens, as they say, and there are times when you need to take the bull by the horns and rise to the occasion. That said, it is also observed that there are people who are invariably seen in Quadrant I. If not, they are in Quadrant III. In fact, they crisscross between Quadrant I and Quadrant III. You seldom see them in Quadrant II and don't even imagine them in Quadrant IV. Literally, their lives are in a constant state of emergency. They do not know how to chill with chamomile tea or relax in a hammock. Words like urgent, rush, got to go, no time, etc. are their common vocabulary. In some sense, that is their tempo, and a few actually thrive in that state of a pumped-up mindset for a while. However, the pernicious effects of over-indulgence in Quadrants I and III are short-fuse temper, insensitivity, mindless execution of tasks, multitasking (aka task switching), meals on-the-go, chaotic diet, and deteriorating health issues, ranging from ulcers, shallow breathing, and chest pains. In short, they don't have the superpower of calmness.

Visionary and respected leaders and achievers have consistently and consciously allocated time to spend in Quadrant II, which is where directions, visions, and planning are formulated and fine-tuned. In fact, the word *solitude* gets its elevated flavour in Quadrant II. Of course, given the demands of daily activities and social interactions, time will also be spent on the other 3 quadrants. Nevertheless, where a concerted amount of time is spent in Quadrant II, calmness and clarity empower that individual. The issue is how much time we should spend in each quadrant and how much time we do *actually* spend in each of the quadrants. A candid *time audit* on our weekly routine would be beneficial in calibrating our True North goals and directions. Needless to say, when too much disproportionate time is spent on quadrants I, III, and/or IV, imbalance, stress, and a sense of emptiness will eventually prevail.

The 80/20 Principle

Vilfredo Pareto[101] was an Italian civil engineer, economist, sociologist, political scientist, and philosopher who contributed significantly during his

---

101 1848-1923, Born in Paris, France, Nationality Italian.

lifetime in the previous century. Among his contributions, he observed and formulated a rather odd mathematical ratio principle, what we now call the Pareto Distribution. As per Pareto, 80% of the wealth in Italy belonged to 20% of the population. This observational principle did not generate much excitement or response until after he passed away. Then, his peers and other researchers started to reconsider the 80/20 principle, and they found its almost ubiquitous application in many other aspects of life, from productivity to customer base and even the clothes you wear.

Today, the 80/20 Principle has taken on a pseudo-cult status in the field of time management and productivity study. Management books espoused it as a time-management utility tool, and Tim Ferriss, in his bestseller *The 4-Hour Work Week*[102], swears by it, and even Richard Koch's book aptly entitled *The 80/20 Principle*[103] has the subtitle *The Secret of Achieving More with Less*. In fact, Richard Koch argued that Pareto's principle had stood the test of time, and essentially it is about achieving more with less and time-management efficiency. Indeed, the 80/20 Principle's almost universally consistent application has vindicated Vilfredo's insightful observation when he was still alive.

Essentially, many things have imbalances when it comes to output and productivity. Apart from wealth distribution, it also applies to *quality losses*. The Romanian-born US industrial engineer Joseph Moses Juran[104] applied the Pareto Principle to his search for high-quality methodology. Way back in 1924, Joseph Juran joined Bell Telephone System and became their quality consultant. He advocated the 80/20 approach to quality control, and at that time, most US industrialists were not able to grasp what he was trying to preach. He then went over to Japan to work with a few corporations there and upgraded the quality of their consumer goods. When the Japanese brands became a worldwide phenomenon from the 70s onwards, only then did the US industry take the Pareto Principle seriously. Today, Dr. Joseph Juran is considered to be the father of many of the quality management techniques. Of the 3 principles in his quality management approach, the first is the Pareto

---

[102] Published 2007.

[103] 2nd edition (2007), Nicholas Brealey Publishing (first published 1997)

[104] 1904-2008. He authored the book "Juran's Quality Control Handbook" (1951), which attracted the attention of JUSE (Japanese Union of Scientists and Engineers), which then invited him to Japan for lectures.

Principle, viz. identifying the vital few and the trivial many. In application, it means identifying the small percentage of root causes in manufacturing or service processes that account for the largest effect in terms of defects or cost.

The legendary IBM applied the Pareto Principle way back in the early 60s and found that about 80% of a computer's time is spent performing about 20% of the operating code. With that insight, IBM then redirected its focus to making its 20% operating code more user-friendly and easier to access, which produced more efficient PCs, demolishing many of its competitors at that time.

Why should we care about the Pareto Principle, and how should we apply it to our daily lives to toughen our minds? Well, to begin with, once properly understood and effectively applied, our daily lives, focus, and productivity will soar, thereby giving our brains the turbocharging they need every day to solve problems and seek innovations. In simple terms, if you can figure out which 20% of your time will give you 80% of your productivity, that is where you should zoom in on your energy and focus. For example, I find that right after my morning exercise and a solid nutritious breakfast (with a strong cup of organic coffee), my brain is at its most productive peak. That is where I do the most challenging mental activity, be it a complex legal submission or a legal issue that requires mind-map solutions.

Just in case you get pedantic over the OCD of the 80/20 ratio, the key takeaway conceptual application is not precise 80/20 quantitative exactness or mathematical precision, but the *"vital few, trivial many"* imbalances awareness that permeates many ethos of applications, from wealth distribution, to engineering defects and even to clients/profits ratio.

Integrating the 3 time-management concepts for synergy.

How do you fit a square into a round hole? Or rather, how do you apply 3 Circles to a 4-quadrant concept, or *vice versa*, to reconcile the 4-Quadrant time management with the 3 Circles, let alone to use the 80/20 mindset to handle the 2 diverging concepts? It's not easy because, fundamentally, there are differing concepts of time management, self-management, and pattern-seeking focus. That said, it is possible if we change our mindset about the *multi-dimensional* platforms these 3 beautiful and powerful concepts sit on.

With the 3 Circles of control/influence/concern, we know that our mind can roam or fluctuate within one of the 3 Circles at any one time, and we know that our Circle of Control is where we are most productive, effective, and centred. Hence, it is the 20% of our productivity centre. Then, we should endeavour to spend 80% of our daily time in the Circle of Control. That is the application of the Pareto Principle to the 3 Circles.

Then, take the 4-Quadrant Time Management. Again, our mind and time can be in any of the 4 quadrants at any one time during the day, and we also know that Quadrant II is where we are most productive and effective, viz., the Zone. With that, the Pareto Principle mandates that we should *prioritise* our time in Quadrant II because it is where our centredness, sense of purpose, and visions/ikigai get reinforced or recalibrated. With regular practice, our sense of calm and productivity output will improve. And with clarity, better decisions are made.

Now looking at the 4 quadrants of Time Management, the 3 Circles can be applied in all 4 situations, and knowing that we are most effective at the Circle of Control, we should endeavour to predominantly focus on that circle in every quadrant that we are engaged in.

Finally, to integrate the trilogy of concepts, we would then endeavour to focus 80% of our prime time and core energy on Quadrant II and mindfully stay within our Circle of Control in that Quadrant as much as possible. That is the sweet spot. Where that can be achieved, our mind would be at its laser-focus optimal state, especially when handling Quadrant I matters. Quadrant II would be the Zone where 'self-actualisation'[105] can be nurtured. You say that you don't have time for Quadrant II, given the daily demands of Quadrants I and III. Well, we make time for the things that matter in our lives. Socrates had so elegantly said a long time ago: *"An unexamined life is not worth living."* And the book called *Essentialism* by Greg McKeown[106] resonates with this imperative, where you gradually trim off all the non-essentials to focus on the

---

[105] Abraham Maslow's highest level in his 5 Hierarchy of Needs. American Psychologist (1908-1970)

[106] Published 2014

essentials. His subtitle is tagged *The Disciplined Pursuit of Less*. This message from Greg McKeown is so timely, too, particularly in our current time of 24/7 internet access and bombardment of social media and push personalised messages/news that are *relevant* to our lives.

"...the basic value proposition of Essentialism: only once you give permission to stop trying to do it all, to stop saying yes to everyone, can you make your highest contribution towards the things that really matter."
– Greg McKeown.

self-actualisation

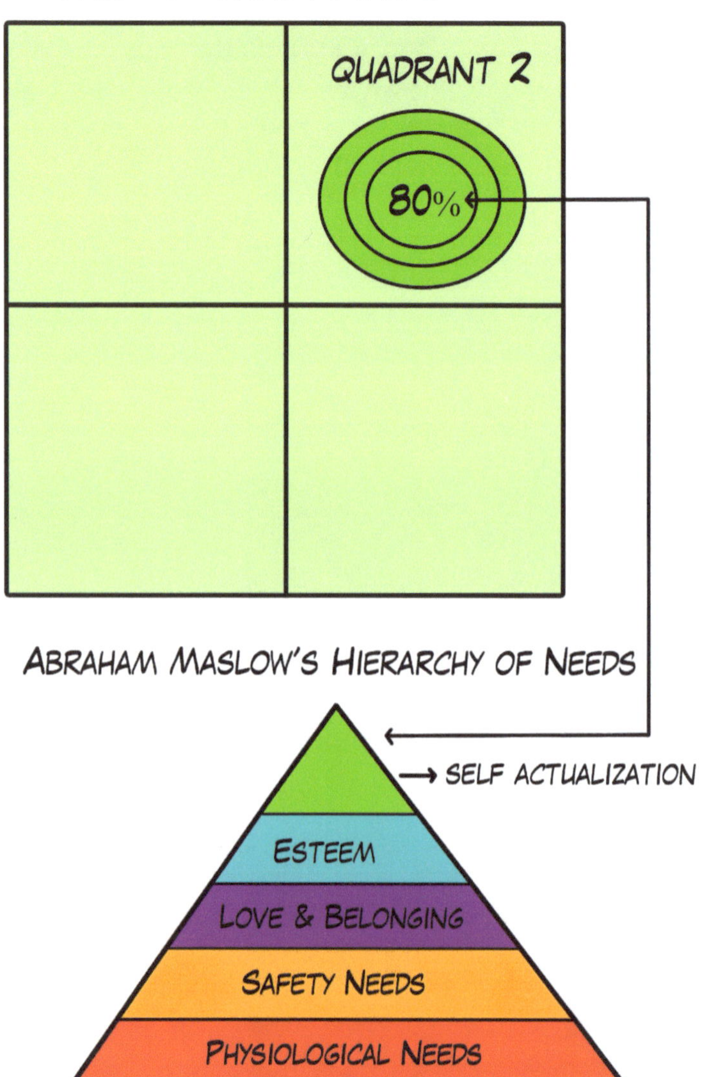

EPILOGUE

L ife is truly a gift. To be able to breathe, to grow, to learn, and to travel and experience the kaleidoscope of experiences, ranging from laughter, sadness, thrills, culinary expeditions, nature exploration, and historical/ architectural wonders are what give life its rich texture.

Now that I am finished writing this book, I want to express my deep appreciation to you, readers, for taking this enriching journey with me in understanding and exploring the power of our brain and mindset, giving directional context to our life journey, optimising social interactions, and cherishing life's fabric of ups and downs, challenges, and victories.

As I conclude this book, the onslaught of megatrends like Generative AI, quantum computing, blockchain, crypto, and big data as the next major disruptors heralds a revolution that is already reshaping our world in unprecedented ways. These transformative technologies are redefining industries, altering the fabric of our economies, and revolutionising how we interact with information and each other. As we stand on the precipice of this new era, it is imperative that we not only acknowledge the potential of these advancements but also prepare to harness their power effectively.

AI, with its capacity to mimic human intelligence and learning, is already making significant inroads into various sectors, from healthcare to finance, driving efficiencies and uncovering new insights at an astonishing pace. Quantum computing, on the other hand, holds the promise of solving problems that are currently beyond the reach of classical computers, potentially unlocking new frontiers in materials science, cryptography, complex system modelling, and even finding a cure for cancer.

Blockchain technology offers a decentralised and secure way to record transactions (aka immutable ledgers), which could revolutionise industries ranging from banking to supply chain management by ensuring transparency and reducing the risk of fraud. Meanwhile, big data analytics enables us to sift through vast amounts of information, uncover patterns, and make data-driven decisions that can drive innovation and growth.

As these technologies converge, they will create synergies that amplify their individual impacts, leading to a cascading effect of innovation and disruption. However, the key to navigating this complex landscape lies not just in understanding these technologies but in having a teachable heart, being adaptive, and applying them effectively in our daily lives and businesses.

That said, my projection is that these disrupters and clusters of revolutionary waves will *not* displace the need for these 10 timeless wisdoms and principles that we have been talking about in the preceding chapters. My take is they will be needed *even more* to manage and moderate these colossal megatrends that are disrupting many industries at an exponential rate.

The other important thing about knowledge and know-how is not that we know about them but that we understand them and are able to internalise and *apply* them in our daily lives. Until and unless we can internalise and apply this wonderful knowledge and strategies, they remain as theories that sit rather nicely on a bookshelf or wall plaques for display only. Or worse, if we misunderstand and/or misapply the knowledge or strategies. It would be like we have been exhaustively and repeatedly chopping a tree with a blunt axe, and someone comes along to offer us a *turbo-charged* chainsaw. We can respond with the following options:

1. No, thank you, we are happy with our blunt axe.
2. Please don't disturb us because we are *so busy* chopping away *productively* with our blunt saw.

3. To acknowledge the generosity of the giver, we say thank you and take the gift of the turbo-charged chainsaw. Then we put it away and got back to the busyness of our blunt axe chopping the tree.
4. We mindlessly take it and use it like a conventional axe.
5. We happily take it and think it is a manual saw. We then use it like a manual saw.
6. We gratefully receive it and open our minds to this new powerful tool. We learn its concept and check out where to charge the battery (wireless version) and how to switch *on* the turbo-charged chainsaw. We test the various speed modes, and we do a trial run of its interaction with various types of wood. Next thing we know, we are adapted to the power and efficiency of the chainsaw, that the blunt saw becomes a redundant or an outdated tool.

The choice is yours to make.

There is an app on our smartphone that allows us to *optimise* our smartphone so that it can function optimally. Some of us even do it daily. The question is: When was the last time you optimised your life? In the end, the 2 key takeaway concepts holding up all the profound strategies are *adaptability* and *teachability*. I wish you well and a happy discovery in this amazing journey called LIFE!

Respect + Namaste,
SK Liow

I hear and I forget,
I see and I remember,
I do and I understand.
– Confucius

APPENDIX

Examples of "Success"

- Get a good job, marry a good spouse, and have wonderful children.
- Earned a Nobel Prize (in any category).
- Delivered a sterling TED Talk.
- Become the CEO of a publicly listed company.
- Established a chain of profitable restaurants or cafes.
- Become the Prime Minister of a country.
- Teach autistic children.
- Solved the global warming problem.
- Find a cure for cancer.
- Recovered from cancer and raised funds for cancer research.
- Travelled to at least xx number of countries in the world.
- Earned a PhD in a complex subject.
- Write a bestseller book.
- Have optimal health and a simple life.
- Have balance in work, hobbies, and relationships.
- Become an expert investor and have multiple streams of passive income to the point where you no longer need to work for the rest of your life.
- Become a super-fit soldier and fight to defend your country.
- Invent something that can benefit the handicapped community.

- Run in every international marathon in the world and touch the finish line.
- Climbed Mount Everest and came back alive.
- Worked with an NGO to help an underdeveloped village in a 3rd world country.
- Learned 5 languages.
- Be an accomplished musician in at least 3 musical instruments.
- Be a happy homemaker and raise healthy and independent children.
- Cruised around the world without worrying about time or money.
- Participate in the Olympics.
- Able to have a morning walk daily and have a cup of tea/coffee with a good friend(s) regularly.
- To be disease-free.
- To be able to take up a completely new skill or study course after retirement.
- To marry your sweetheart.
- To have a child or many children.
- Managed to solve the Israel-Palestine conflict.
- To be able to have great-grandchildren and play with them.
- To be debt-free.
- To be able to fly a plane.
- To be alive every day (after recovering from a near-death illness or accident).
- To raise funds for charity and remain anonymous.
- Have a marvellous recipe for a dish that is taking the locality or country by storm.
- To travel to outer space.
- To compete in and complete the Ironman race or the triathlon.
- To be able to sleep peacefully every night.
- To be happy.
- To hear both your parents tell their friends that they are so proud of their child (you).
- Able to read your favourite book over a cup of latte or your favourite wine, and stress-free.

- To own your favourite dream car.
- To have children hugging you in gratitude after you teach them some life skills.
- To be able to expose a corrupt regime.
- To understand the meaning of self-actualisation as per Abraham Maslow's hierarchy of needs and to be at that level.
- To be able to have dinner with your all-time favourite movie star or TV personality.
- To win the grand prize of the state lottery.
- To have nutritious food on the table, 3 times a day, every day.
- To be respected as a community leader.
- To be able to sing and win in the national talent show.
- To be able to solve the global warming crisis.
- To be able to chill in a hammock, relaxing with jazz music and your favourite drink.
- To be able to walk after a major car accident.
- To have a happy and close-knit family.